—— *THE SERVANT-SON* ——

Donald Coggan was Archbishop of Canterbury from 1974 to 1980. He is the author of many books, on subjects ranging from theology and biblical studies to biography and spirituality; his most recent title was *The Voice from the Cross* (Triangle 1993). He now lives in Winchester with his wife Jean. They have two daughters.

D0994211

Also by Donald Coggan and published by Triangle:
Voice from the Cross, Triangle 1993

The
SERVANT-SON

JESUS THEN AND NOW

Donald Coggan

TRI∆NGLE

First published in Great Britain 1995
Triangle
Society for Promoting Christian Knowledge
Holy Trinity Church
Marylebone Road
London NW1 4DU

British Library Cataloguing-in-Publication Data
A catalogue record for this book is available from the British Library

ISBN 0-281-04802-9

Typeset by Dorwyn Ltd, Rowlands Castle, Hants
Printed and bound in Great Britain by
BPC Paperbacks Ltd
Member of The British Printing Company Ltd

For Jean—
loved companion and colleague for sixty years.

Contents

'Jesus, well aware that . . . he had come from God and was going back to God . . . took off his outer garment and, taking a towel, tied it round him.'

(John 13.3–4)

Enjoy yourself. Why not? Bible study is for discovery and enjoyment. To some groups and to some individuals it is a bore—so the group breaks up or the individual gives up.

But why should it be a bore? It is surprising that it can be, for at the heart of the Bible is the figure of a young man who, on any reckoning, created a shattering sensation in his short lifetime. He was dynamic, controversial, forceful, tender, deeply loved, bitterly hated . . . He is the key to the meaning of the Bible.

If we could meet him, see him more clearly, there would be no boredom on our part. That is the purpose of this book—to see him as he *was*, the Servant-Son of God; to know him as he *is*, now, today, always.

Enjoy yourself as you get to work. You are embarking on a voyage of discovery. Do not rush. Chew the cud slowly, like a good cow! You might want to read the book fairly rapidly at the start (see the next pages for its plan) and then come back and read it chapter by chapter, or section by section, stopping where you want to as you go along. Make your own decisions. If at the end you feel yourself more surely on the Christian road, then, as *My Fair Lady* put it, 'wouldn't it be luverly'!

Donald Coggan
Winchester

The Plan
of the Book

There are nine chapters. This is what they are about:

—— 1 FORMATIVE YEARS ——

The chapter introduces us to some of the influences which went to the making of Jesus' personality and outlook—his mother Mary, Joseph, the Jerusalem temple, the local synagogue, his home, and the workshop where he earned his living. It examines the atmosphere which surrounded him. (pp. 1–15)

—— 2 BAPTISM ——

We meet two men, very different in character the one from the other—John the baptizer, and Jesus from Nazareth. What happened to Jesus at his baptism? What 'came over' him? (pp. 16–23)

—— 3 TEMPTATION ——

The forty days in the wilderness constituted a terrible ordeal for Jesus—a kind of wrestling match with evil. What was it all about? What was the point of it? He won—but how? (pp. 24–34)

——— 4 SUFFERING SERVANT ———

We go to the prophet Isaiah to study certain passages (called 'servant songs') which Jesus often read and which were influential in forming the pattern of his ministry—they defined its nature and pointed to its climax. (pp. 35–49)

——— 5 FIRST SERMON ———

We watch Jesus publicly setting out his programme—'if you want to know what my ministry is about, listen to this.' We note his declaration of intent. (pp. 50–57)

——— 6 MINISTER OF HEALTH ———

Jesus was a *minister* in the sense that he cared for the needs of others, rather than for his own needs. He was a minister of *health* in the widest sense of the word—restoration, re-creation, wholeness, holiness. We watch him doing battle with people's three great enemies—ignorance, sin, and disease. We listen to him teaching and preaching, and we study examples of his healing work. (pp. 58–76)

——— 7 DRAMATIST ———

Jesus taught not only by the use of *words*, reaching us through our ears. He taught also by the use of *drama*, reaching us through our eyes and through the use of our imagination. (pp. 77–93)

——— 8 SERVANT-SON CHURCH ———

Jesus was the Messiah, the one anointed by God to fulfil a certain task. This he did by being the Servant-Son even to death. 'As the Father sent me, so I send you.' The church is here to continue that task, though in different circumstances and under different conditions. (pp. 94–106)

9 *JESUS—THEN AND NOW*

Jesus *then*—the first eight chapters have been concerned with him as a human being—and more. What is our attitude to Jesus *now*? 'Thanks for the memory'? Is that all? Or is there more to it—to him—than that? If so, of what does the 'more' consist? (pp. 107–121)

Each chapter is followed by questions, aimed to elicit further thought.

Each chapter is followed by prayers, for Bible study which does not issue in prayer is a poor thing.

All that is needed for our work is a Bible, preferably in a modern translation. The *Revised English Bible* is recommended (Oxford University Press and Cambridge University Press, 1989).

A notebook at the ready—for findings, questions, etc.—will help.

Formative Years

In this chapter, we examine the background of the life of Jesus in the years before his public ministry began, and the influences which moulded his character.

The following are some of the most important references:

Mary—**Luke 1.26–38**
Joseph—**Matthew 1.18ff.**
Temple—**Luke 2.41–52**
Synagogue—**Luke 4.14–22** (on this, see more fully Chapter 5, First Sermon)

'When Jesus began his work he was about thirty years old.' 'Dear doctor Luke', as Paul calls Luke the evangelist, liked to get his facts right. He sets the ministry of John the baptizer firmly in the context of local political and ecclesiastical VIPs (**Luke 3.1–2**). When he moves on to introduce Jesus as a public figure, he tells us that he was no irresponsible youngster; on the contrary, 'he began his [public] work when he was about thirty years old.' (**Luke 3.23**) How interesting! But how tantalizing! Luke had been at pains to devote the best part of two long chapters to the events which surrounded Jesus' birth, to Elizabeth, to Joseph and Mary, to the birth itself, to the circumcision of the infant boy, to the aged Simeon and Anna—and then, *silence* up to Jesus' public appearance at the mature age of thirty. (There is one exception to this silence: it is the story of the visit of the holy family to Jerusalem when Jesus was about twelve years old. To this we shall come later: see pp. 5–8).

No wonder that writers have called these three decades 'the hidden years' in the life of Jesus, and have sought, often with more imagination than is justified, to penetrate the darkness. This desire is the more excusable because, as we readily recognize in our own lives and in the lives of our contemporaries, these years are formative. A man is not made overnight. He is formed—and fashioned gradually—in the womb and in the first decades of his life. In these years, through storm and struggle, through the joys and pains of adolescence and young manhood, decisions are made, patterns of lifestyle and conduct are established, ideals are formed, heroes are worshipped and dethroned, life's-work is decided on. There is every reason to believe that for Jesus these factors were as determinative, as powerful, as for any other boy, as he worked his way through to the maturity of manhood.

Though, as we have seen, the *incidents* of those years are minimal as given to us in the Gospels, we are not left in such deep darkness as we might at first fear. There were influences at work, there were institutions and 'atmospheres', all of which had their bearing, some powerful, some less so, in the formation of Jesus the Christ—things which *made* him the preacher, healer, teacher that he came to be. It will be time well spent to examine these influences and not to hurry over that examination. I mention five.

2

——— MARY ———

If Matthew, in his stories of the infancy of Jesus, focuses his attention on the person of Joseph (**Matthew 1.18–25**), Luke concentrates on the person of Mary. He is expert in telling a story. He is a doctor with a deep sensitivity. With great delicacy he looks at the conception and birth of Jesus as it were through the eyes of Mary, and enters into the troubled wonder with which she greeted the fact of her pregnancy. The angel seeks to reassure her—'Greetings, most favoured one! The Lord is with you.' But Mary is troubled—what does that greeting mean? 'Do not be afraid, Mary, for God has been gracious to you.' The bewilderment persists—'How can this be? I am still a virgin.' Then, deep within her comes the conviction that she is not alone—'The Holy Spirit will come upon you, and the power of the Most High will overshadow you . . . God's promises can never fail.' (**Luke 1.35–37**) It was like the calm which comes after a storm has blown itself out. Mary's reply is the more powerful for its superb simplicity: 'I am the Lord's servant; may it be as you have said.'

'The Lord's *servant*.' Here is Mary as the Servant-Mother. Hold on to that reply and ponder it. For it may be that it gives us a clue—*the* clue?—to the meaning of her son's life and death. The Servant-Mother was about to bear him who, above all others, was to be the servant of the Lord.

Who knows the influence of a mother on her unborn child? Here is a world of mystery which is still not wholly understood. But is it not possible that something of the concept of dedicated servanthood which was at the very heart of this young pregnant woman 'got through' to the child as yet unborn, and became an integral part in the shaping of his manhood and his ministry? There may be more in this than has been generally recognized.

Be that as it may, of this we may be certain: Mary saw, with a God-given clarity, at the moment of her greatest crisis, that *servanthood* lies at the very centre of the meaning of life as God intends it to be lived. Servanthood, obedience, in the great crises of life and in the little decisions of everyday, Mary saw as things of first importance. And so she doubtless taught the little boy on her lap, at her knee, through all his formative years. What greater prayer could she offer for her son than that he might grow up to be a servant of the Lord—possibly (did she glimpse it as she pondered on these things in her heart?) he might be even *the* servant of the Lord.

One of the greatest gifts that a mother can give to her children is not only to pray for them but, from their earliest years, to teach them to pray. We may be sure that Mary's little boy was not very old when he began to pray the prayer which his mother used when first she knew she was pregnant: 'I am the Lord's servant; may it be to me as you have said', or, to put it more simply and shortly, 'Your will be done'. As the boy grew older, she taught him what it meant to think of God as king, to see life lived under his kingship as the only life worth living. She taught him to pray: 'Your kingdom come'. Out of her own experience of life and prayer, she learned to pray. Out of that same experience she taught her son to pray: 'Your kingdom come, your will be done', and to do so, not grudgingly but exultingly.

It is not stretching our imagination too far to suggest that we owe to Mary those two basic clauses which come at the beginning of her son's prayer—'Your kingdom come, your will be done'.

What a debt we owe her!

—— JOSEPH ——

Matthew introduces Joseph to us as 'a man of principle' (**Matthew 1.19**), a just, honest, good man; and a sensitive man who 'wanted to save [Mary] from exposure'. We know little else about him directly. But it is surely significant that when Jesus, in his public ministry, had to decide what were the main ways in which he was to teach his hearers about God, he chose to speak of him as *father* and as king. Of the kingship of God we need say nothing at this point, though we have suggested that Mary may have had a share in forming that concept in her son's mind. But why did Jesus put so much emphasis on the *father*hood of God?

The first reason is obvious: the Scriptures with which Jesus became familiar from his earliest days (see Synagogue section, pp. 8–9) often referred to God as father—both in a national sense (for example: 'Have we not all one father? Did not one God create us?' [**Malachi 2.10**]), and in a more personal sense (for example: 'As a father has compassion on his children, so the Lord has compassion on those who fear him' [**Psalm 103.13**]). It was natural, then, that

4

Jesus should take up, expand, and develop this biblical insight into the character of God. Israel's redeemer was the nation's father.

But we may believe that the second reason for the centrality of God's fatherhood in the teaching of Jesus was the man who, though not in the physical sense his father, stood in that relationship to him and was the head of the household of which Jesus was a member. The character of Joseph was such that Jesus saw no incongruity in moving mentally from the fatherhood of Joseph to the fatherhood of God. For Joseph, in his character—a 'man of principle', a sensitive, caring man—reflected in his own person what we conceive to be most Godlike in the character of the Almighty and, more particularly, in the way that that character relates to his sons and daughters. There was no contradiction in thinking in terms of fatherhood and of kingship when Jesus sought to conceive of God and to teach about him. In his God, caring love (fatherhood) and authority (kingship) met in a holy and magnificent alliance.

Mary taught the growing boy to think of himself as a *servant*, living in loving obedience to God. Joseph taught him to think of himself as a *son* entering into a relationship which grew ever more intimate as youth gave way to adult life. Servant and son: there was no limit to the richness of that concept, first for Jesus himself and then for those he taught.

—— *TEMPLE* ——

'It was the practice of his parents to go to Jerusalem *every year* for the Passover festival; and when he was twelve, they made the pilgrimage *as usual*.' (Luke 2.41–42, author's italics)

For the modern traveller, the journey from Nazareth in the north to Jerusalem, the capital, in the south is an easy one: it can be done by car in a matter of a few hours. But in the days when it had to be done by donkey, or on foot, the journey was a considerable one. There were dangers to be met—brigands abounded and it was wisest to travel in companies. There were provisions to be planned—for beasts and humans. It was quite an undertaking. But it could be fun, especially for the young. There was the sense of festivity—not for nothing were the religious festivals called feasts. There was the thrill of the unknown or, at least, of the unfamiliar. And at the end of the journey there was the climb and the sheer marvel of seeing Jerusalem, the city of which the poets had sung and the religious had dreamed. At the heart of it all was the temple, its buildings shimmering in the sunlight. No wonder one of the rabbis had said that he who had not seen the temple had not lived.

At the first glimpse of that temple, the pulse of the young boy Jesus must have raced. As he went up year after year, wonder at the architecture of the building gave way to something deeper, something akin to awe (I can still recall my first visit to St Paul's Cathedral in London—its echoing vastness had a dimension greater than the architectural; it had about it something of the numinous—there was an element of the mysterious which was awe-inspiring). Jesus must have been asked whether the glory of the temple reflected in some way the magnificence of the God who was at least supposed to be the centre of its worship. Boyish excitement began to give place to adolescent awe.

It was a place for the asking of questions. There in the temple courts, teaching went on. In the full flood of his public ministry, Jesus was himself to do much teaching work there. As a boy of twelve years old he found himself at the listening end and was no doubt entranced to be a pupil. Luke gives us a delightful thumbnail sketch of the boy 'sitting in the temple surrounded by the teachers, listening to them and putting questions' (Luke 2.46). His sharp intelligence amazed the authorized teachers; they had never seen it before quite in this fashion. As he trudged back to his home town and, when the time came, as he worked at the carpenter's bench, Jesus' mind ran back over those sessions of question and answer in the temple. Awe and wonder led him on to worship.

And yet—he was puzzled. Big questions raised their heads, and the boy did not find readily available those who had the answer or even those who shared his perplexity.

For example, the very plan on which the temple was based raised questions in the boy's developing mind. Why was there this series of courts within the temple locality? There was the big outer one into which anyone, irrespective of nationality, was allowed free entrance. That was all right. But why was there this notice threatening death to any non-Jew who ventured through that 'middle wall of partition' and entered the Jewish court? It was a man-made division. What did God think about that? Should there not be equal access for Jew and non-Jew alike into the holy place? Did nationality matter to God? Or did that wall savour of a kind of religious apartheid? There was yet another division, an equally stern refusal of access. The high priest alone, and that only once a year, and then only under the strictest conditions, was allowed to pass from the holy Jewish court into the most holy place of all. This puzzled Titus, the Roman governor, when in AD 70 he was destroying the temple. He had expected to find a statue of the Jewish God—all the religions he had met had images of their gods. But when Titus broke through to the most holy place, he found—nothing (except the ark of the covenant)! To a *Jew* this was to be expected; it was obviously right, for their prophets had inveighed again and again against the stupidity of making images of the deity (see, for example, **Isaiah 44.9–20**). But Titus found it incomprehensible.

The architectural plan raised problems which the young Jesus found hard to resolve. And if the plan of the buildings was problematical, what went on in the area raised even more questions in his mind. Why all these sacrifices—daily, and in greater number at the festivals? Why all this slaughtering of beasts and birds? Why all the stench of ever-flowing blood, the burning of the fires, the carving up of the beasts? There was something to be said for the architecture and for the sacrificial system. No sinner should rush into the divine presence without pause and without preparation. Something must be done about each person's defilement; the nasty reality of sin must be faced. The series of courts, the continuing offering of sacrifices spoke of the otherness of God and the soiled nature of men and women, and the need to face the reality and the consequences of these facts. That was all on the positive side. Israel had a word to say to the world on those issues.

But there were other and deeper questions which assaulted the mind of the growing boy. Granted the otherness, the awe-fulness, of Israel's God; granted the folly, even the danger, of rushing thoughtlessly and unprepared into his presence; this majestic God was also a father who yearned for his children to be near him and never to abandon that closeness. The sacrifices might point to the otherness of God, but what could they *effect*? Was the time coming, was it virtually come, when sacrifices had achieved their purpose and were needed no more?

His mind went rushing on. Did the temple, which had thrilled him when first he saw it and which had spoken its message to his own heart, always speak of the glory of God and point to him? Or was it sometimes a monument to human megalomania? Could it be a hollow shrine, bereft of the presence of the God in whose name it had been erected? Later, when Jesus was drawing near to the end of his public ministry, he was to have some very hard things to say about these matters. Can we doubt that the seeds of that thinking were sown in his visits to the temple in the years of his adolescence and young manhood?

——— SYNAGOGUE ———

The synagogue was a remarkable institution and was of basic importance in the maintenance of Jewish life and worship. As Jews, for reasons of persecution or of the propagation of trade and industry, spread throughout the Graeco–Roman world, so synagogues sprang up in city after city. Wherever ten Jewish males were present, there it was possible to establish a synagogue. The word essentially means a 'gathering together' and itself points to the variety of uses to which it was put. It was primarily a place of corporate worship and prayer and for the reading of the Jewish Scriptures. It was also a place of instruction where the Jewish faith was expounded and the Jewish way of life explained—it is interesting that the Yiddish word for synagogue is *schul* which derives from the Old High German *scuola*, school. There, too, justice was dispensed and cases decided. Especially after the destruction of the temple in AD 70, synagogues served as a kind of cement holding together the scattered pieces of Jewish life.

But before AD 70, in the lifetime of Jesus, the synagogue was a powerful influence, not only abroad but within the land of Israel itself. We need not doubt that it influenced Jesus. Luke tells us that it was Jesus' regular habit to go to the synagogue on the sabbath day (**Luke 4.16**). Indeed he took his part in the leadership of its worship—'He stood up to read the lesson'. He would have found in the worship of his local synagogue the intimacy of a local gathering of like-minded Jews, which contrasted, not always to its own disadvantage, with the awe-inspiring majesty of the temple services in Jerusalem.

Here in the synagogue Jesus learnt more about prayer. His mother had begun to teach him the essence of personal devotion—'I am the Lord's servant; may it be as you have said'. Now he was to see the meaning of *public* worship and corporate prayer; the Psalms became his textbook. Here, again, he was to hear the Scriptures read and expounded; here he met with the great figures of his national story who, as he listened, seemed to emerge from the pages and stride across his imagination—Abraham, Isaac, Jacob, Moses; the prophets, such as Jeremiah, Amos, Hosea, and Isaiah with his 'servant songs' (see Chapter 4). Here great concepts began to form in his mind and to impinge on his conscience—the holiness and majesty of God, his love and justice, the difference between right and wrong without which no society and no individual could find wholeness. His mind was stretched, his imagination fired, his heart stirred.

Sometimes, as he heard those Scriptures read and expounded, he found them a window into heaven. Sometimes, no doubt, he found the teaching dull, his keen powers of perception aching for something deeper. He took the bad with the good, the inspired with the banal, and, in the quiet of the hills or at work at the carpenter's bench, the sorting process went on and the boy's character was made. We shall see later that the Scriptures were his strength and stay in times of temptation and of suffering, and that the synagogue was the place to which he constantly went when, in his public ministry, his turn came to be the teacher.

——— HOME AND WORKSHOP ———

We have suggested, at the beginning of this chapter, that the influence of his mother on the infant and boy Jesus must have been profound. Mary shared with him her sense of obedience, and of servanthood. Indeed, in doing so she may have sown the seed which was to become the dominating concept of his life and ministry. The bond between mother and son must have been very close and their love for one another very deep. They shared exile in Egypt (**Matthew 2.13ff.**). They shared danger when an angry crowd tried to throw the young preacher over the cliff—for who can doubt that the mother was there to hear her son's first sermon in the synagogue at Nazareth? (**Luke 4.28–30**) These things brought them closer together as the years went by. And at the end, the mother was there as the son spent those long hours hanging on the cross (**John 19.25ff.**).

But it wasn't all easy—at least so the Gospels seem to say. There was that occasion when the adolescent boy had stayed behind in Jerusalem without telling his parents—'My son', his mother said, 'Why have you treated us like this?' (**Luke 2.48**) And *he* had had to rebuke *her* at the wedding feast when the wine supply ran out. 'Woman', he said. Woman? To our ears the word sounds unbearably harsh—so much so that J. B. Phillips and the *Revised English Bible* refuse to translate it at all. The *New English Bible* translates the word (but it is not a translation!) 'mother'. Perhaps 'my dear mother' would be nearest to the truth, if the words were said in a tone of good-tempered but none the less sincere rebuke, rather as we say in protestation at some misunderstanding—'my dear *fellow!*' 'My dear *mother*, my hour has not yet come.' Tenderly said, no doubt. But it was none the less a rebuke. She had not understood (**John 2.1ff.**).

We can appreciate this. This astonishing young man, whom she had watched growing up from his infancy, was becoming more than Mary could comprehend. Let us face it, it cannot have been easy to see him growing, if not away from her, beyond her. There was the occasion when he kept her waiting outside the house while he was teaching inside. She and his brothers sent in a message. He replied: 'Who are my mother and my brothers? Here are my mother and my brothers. Whoever does the will of God is my brother and sister and *mother*.' (**Mark 3.31–35**, author's italics) There were tensions— obedience to the absolute demands of the heavenly father does not always make earthly relationships easy or comfortable.

His brothers and sisters? There came a time when they thought Jesus was crazy, and were not slow to say so. There were James and Joses and Judas and Simon and unnamed sisters as well (**Mark 6.3**). With an almost brutal frankness, Mark tells of a time when 'his family . . . set out to take charge of him. "He is out of his mind", they said.' (**Mark 3.21**) Was there an element of jealousy here, as they watched the crowds gathering round Jesus and pressing in on him? What was the secret of his success and popularity? Why did people throw over their life's-work and follow him? Why did he spend so much time in prayer, away from the madding crowd? Why all this talk of God's reign and this intimacy of contact with his *Abba*-God? It was all a bit beyond them—and tensions resulted in the rough and tumble of family life. If misunderstandings are painful, they are doubly so when they occur within the family circle.

Then there was the workshop, the wider world of trade and commerce—and that in a country overrun by a hated foreign power. Rome always found relations with Israel difficult—at any moment a rebellion might blow up in the face of the local governor. Pontius Pilate and his ilk did not find an assignment to that part of the empire an easy one. Rome needed Palestine on strategic and military and economic grounds. If it found dissent—and how the Jews hated those Roman standards with their blasphemous inscriptions!—then that dissent must be crushed. Taxes must be imposed and paid—or else!

First-century Palestine was a stormy place in which to earn a living. But no one could say it was uninteresting. From time immemorial this little strip of land had been one of the great trade routes through which the caravans passed, bringing news from afar with their goods. The Decapolis (the ten cities) was not far away—Greek was spoken there and it is likely that Jesus picked up a smattering of that lovely language and sniffed the scent of exciting thought forms wider than those of his own people. There were ethnic tensions, and religious tensions which made themselves felt in and around the workshop at Nazareth where he earned his living and, no doubt, contributed to the upkeep of his family.

It was not all tension in the workshop. Those long years at the carpenter's bench provided the young man with a challenge to which he gladly responded. Work was good, demanding, creative. The possibility of producing what was shoddy presented itself every day—and was there to be resisted! Who can imagine a table ill-balanced or a yoke which irked the neck of an ox ever coming out of the Nazareth workshop? If, as he gradually came to see, Jesus was a fellow-worker with his father (see, for example, **John 5.17**), that unity of work and purpose applied not only to the future ministry of preaching, teaching, and healing, but to the work done at the bench with hammer and lathe and nails. There was a challenge there which he relished. There could be no divide between sacred and secular.

The workshop presented him, too, with an opportunity to get to know human nature in all its infinite variety—the wretchedness of grinding poverty, the dishonesty of unpaid accounts, the sharpness of a hard-driven bargain, the goodness of generosity or of a joke shared over the counter. Humour and pathos, meanness and no-bility, bitterness and greatness—there is not much about human nature that you do not meet in a decade or two spent in the business world. It all provided Jesus with insights into the secrets of men and women and into an understanding of their very nature which was to stand him in good stead when he preached to the thousands or ministered 'to a mind diseased', seeking to 'cleanse the stuff'd bosom of that perilous stuff which weighs upon the heart'.

Luke makes the point that 'the child (Jesus) grew big and strong and full of wisdom; and God's favour was upon him.' (Luke 2.40) He underlines this a few verses later: 'As Jesus grew he advanced in wisdom and in favour with God and men.' (Luke 2.52) If that was true of his boyhood and adolescence, we may believe that such growth continued during the business years of his young manhood.

Mary and Joseph and temple and synagogue and home and workshop—all had made their contribution to the making of this man. He was a man rich in experience of God and of men and women who, at the age of about thirty, emerged from the compara-tive hiddenness of Nazareth into the full glare of his public life and ministry. Highly gifted, richly experienced—how were these gifts to be used, how were these riches to be shared? Those were the basic questions which faced him.

Before those questions were answered, two events were to take place which would be crucial to their answering: his baptism and his temptation.

—— *QUESTIONS* ——

1 This chapter has attempted to picture Jesus up to the age of about thirty. The Epistle to the Hebrews says he was 'tested in every way as we are, only without sinning.' (**Hebrews 4.15**) What does this suggest as to the reality of the manhood of Jesus?

2 'I am the Lord's servant; may it be as you have said.' (**Luke 1.38**) How would you describe Mary's prayer—'submission'? Can you find a better word?

3 God as father. Can you find in the Bible references which point to the motherlike character of God?

4 The synagogue and the temple were meant as meeting-places with God. Both had their strengths and their weaknesses. Have they any relevance to your local church and worship?

5 The section on the temple (pp. 5–8 above) points out that its plan accentuated the difference between Jews and Gentiles in their approach to God. Paul deals with this problem in **Ephesians 2.11–18**. How does he see the solution of the problem?

———— PRAYERS ————

We pray for those bringing up the young—
>   *parents*
>   *teachers*
>   *club leaders.*

We pray for those who write what young people read
>   *create their radio and television programmes*
>   *lead their worship*
that through their guidance, the young will fill their thoughts with what is
>   *true and noble*
>   *just and pure*
>   *lovable and attractive.*

We pray for homes where only one parent is present
>   *where stress reigns*
where poverty denies the fulness of life which is God's plan for all.

We pray for those who have no work
>   *who lack the ordered rhythm of labour and rest.*
Spirit of the living God,
>   *guide them*
>   *hold them*
>   *bless them.*

>   *Jesus, Lord and Brother,*
>   *who in Nazareth grew to manhood,*
>   *busy in the sunlit workshop*
>   *with eye and hand and brain,*
>   *yet dreaming of a kingdom to be built—*
>   *worldwide, eternal, not made with hands:*
>   *Help us to grow in wisdom,*
>   *loving the things of heaven,*
>   *seeing the world as with your eyes,*

at its true value:
for your sake, our Saviour Jesus Christ.[1]

Almighty God, our heavenly Father,
who gave marriage to be a source of blessing to mankind,
we thank you for the joys of family life.
May we know your presence and peace in our homes;
fill them with your love,
and use them for your glory;
through Jesus Christ our Lord.[2]

Baptism

In this chapter, we meet two men—John the baptizer and Jesus the baptized. We seek to understand what his baptism meant to Jesus in view of his coming ministry.

On the baptizer, read **Matthew 3.1–12**

On Jesus at his baptism, read **Matthew 3.13–17**

Note also **John 3.25–30**

Psalm 2.2–9

Isaiah 42.1–9

The formative hidden years were at an end—perhaps not quite so hidden as some might have thought who had not taken into consideration the factors dealt with in the previous chapter. But they were years when there was no glare of publicity focusing on the young man at Nazareth, though, no doubt, people were beginning to comment on and ask questions about one who, to say the least, was unusual.

But before Jesus finally emerged from comparative obscurity into public ministry, two events were to take place which were to influence radically the nature of his ministry. It would not be too much to say that they were formative in the shaping of that ministry. The material had been collecting for three decades; it needed these events to set that material alight, to cause it to burst into flame. Those events were the baptism of Jesus, and his temptation in the wilderness.

The first event was closely connected with a man, John the baptizer. We must glance at him for a moment.

───── *JOHN THE BAPTIZER* ─────

A cousin of Jesus—John's mother was a kinswoman of Mary the mother of Jesus—John presents a strange figure in the pages of the gospels. Rough and rugged, he was full of truth if not of grace! Dressed in a rough coat of camel's hair to resist the biting cold of winter winds, with a leather belt round his waist, and feeding on what nature could provide for him (locusts and wild honey), he had all the marks of an Old Testament prophet (**Mark 1.2ff.**). As people listened to his tough, unpolished words, they were reminded of what one of their prophets had said: 'I am about to send my messenger to clear a path before me. Suddenly the Lord whom you seek will come to his temple . . .' (**Malachi 3.1**). Was this what Isaiah had meant when he wrote: 'Clear a road through the wilderness for the Lord, prepare a highway across the desert for our God' (**Isaiah 40.3**)? Certainly this man did not mince his words; no man seeking popular acclaim would address his audience as 'viper's brood'! They had all seen a forest fire and watched the snakes wriggle their way out from it and down to the saving waters: they took his point! He would not stand for any pious language or emotional crowd response—'*Prove* your repentance', he said (**Luke 3.8**, author's italics). Nor should they trust in family or racial superiority. It was no use their saying, 'We have Abraham for our father'—there is no life in a religion like that; its destiny is destruction by fire. When the crowds asked him what were they to do, the reply was unequivocal—'Whoever has two shirts must share with him who has none, and whoever has food must do the same.' To the tax gatherers accustomed to adding a little extra for themselves he said 'Exact no more than the assessment.' To the soldiers: 'No bullying; no blackmail; make do with your pay!' This was no time for the 'consolations of religion', nor was the baptizer the man to dispense such consolations. Judgement was round the corner. John was a voice crying out. Content to be that and nothing more, he pointed to someone the straps of whose shoes he felt himself unworthy to unfasten. The ministry of that coming one he saw in terms of judgement and of fire which would burn up the unreal, the pseudo-religion, the chaff. We can hear the raucous voice, we can see the fiery eyes. John the baptizer was tough.

At the same time there was about him an element of the sublime. He was *content* to be a voice, a finger-post pointing away from himself to one greater than he. He himself was not the bridegroom; he was simply the best man. He shrank from any suggestion that he was the central figure on the stage. The Messiah, the Christ, the anointed, Jesus—'*He* must grow greater; I must become less' (**John 3.30**, author's italics).

Such was the man to whom Jesus came to receive baptism at his hands. Matthew alone of the evangelists tells of John's hesitation and of his attempt to dissuade Jesus from such an action. 'Do *you* come to *me*? It is I who need to be baptized by you.' (**Matthew 3.14–15**, author's italics). The objection was natural enough, and the recording of it perhaps reflected an unease on the part of members of the early church who questioned why a sinless Jesus should share in a rite which was for the forgiveness of sins. But the reply of Jesus to the baptizer's objection is deeply significant: 'Let it be so for the present; it is right for us to do all that God requires.' The crucial word in that reply is '*us*'. Jesus does not stand apart from the dirty crowd. He is no aloof figure, looking down on his contemporaries. No; here at the lowest point of the earth's surface on the banks of the River Jordan *he stands in with them*—'It is right for *us* . . .'. He is one with them.

—— *JESUS THE BAPTIZED* ——

We turn now from John the baptizer to Jesus the baptized. It is clear that all the evangelists who give us the story of Jesus' baptism by John saw that the main actor by the Jordan that day was neither of these two men, but was *God himself*—'The Spirit of God descending as a dove'. Mark, with a typically graphic touch, adds that Jesus, 'as he was coming up out of the water, saw the heavens open'—which, presumably, was his way of saying that here was a divine revelation: God speaking, God at work at a point in history, in a geographical locality, to and through the man of his choice.

'Like a dove'. The dove to a Jew was the symbol of peace, gentleness, reconciliation. Was this an indication of the essential nature of the ministry which Jesus was to exercise? Would John have preferred a flame of fire to descend on Jesus' head? Later on, when John was in prison, he wondered whether after all the man to whom he had so faithfully pointed was in fact the one who was to come. He, the baptizer, had spoken of a fiery figure cutting down fruitless trees and throwing them on the flames—but here was a dove-like man, a man of peace and reconciliation. We can understand his perplexity (**Matthew 11.2–6**).

But the imagery of the dove, suggestive as it is, is secondary in importance to 'the voice from heaven' to which all three evangelists refer and whose words they record. Let us look at these words carefully: 'This is my beloved Son, in whom I take delight' (**Matthew 3.17**); 'You are my beloved Son; in you I take delight' (**Mark 1.11**); 'You are my beloved Son; in you I delight (**Luke 3.22**). This clearly reflects Psalm 2—a royal psalm used at the time of coronation, where God is depicted as saying: 'I myself have enthroned my king on Zion, my holy mountain' (**Psalm 2.6**) and saying to that king: 'You are my son.' (**Psalm 2.7**) So the words from heaven 'This is (you are) my beloved Son' designate Jesus as king and son. That is the nature of his being. One cannot speak in loftier terms than these—God's *son*. (We should note that the designation of Jesus as God's beloved son is repeated at the transfiguration. See **Mark 9.7**.)

There is another passage in the Old Testament which is echoed in these words from heaven: 'Here is my servant, whom I uphold, my chosen one, in whom I take delight.' (Isaiah 42.1) This verse introduces the first of the four 'servant songs' to which we shall come in Chapter 4. Suffice it to say here that these poems introduce us to a mysterious figure, the *servant* of the Lord, whose character is sketched for us in passages which reach their climax in the great passion poem of **Isaiah 52.14–53.12**.

In these words in the Gospels, redolent of **Psalm 2** and **Isaiah 42**, we have the picture of a kingly-*son* and of a *servant* of the Lord, in a strange and wonderful conjunction. *That* is the spirit which descended on this young man at the time of his baptism. Are the two concepts self-contradictory? Or is it possible that they could be joined together in a ministry such as had never been seen before? Could the majesty of sonship be married to the humiliation of servanthood? Is it possible that the kingly-sonship could best be seen— could *only* be seen?—*in and through* servanthood? Those are the questions posed at Jesus' baptism by the voice from heaven, posed with a clarity which brooked no denial but which would have to be worked out in an agony of testing. To the beginning of that testing, to the temptation in the wilderness, we now turn.

—— *QUESTIONS* ——

1 John the baptizer was a Mr Valiant-for-Truth who 'cleared a road through the wilderness for the Lord'. Name some modern instances of similar men and women, and think about them. Where does moral courage come in our scale of values?

2 John spoke of coming judgement. We moderns are shy about speaking of God's anger. Are we right or wrong in this?

3 'The main actor . . . was God himself.' What do the stories of Jesus' baptism tell us of the person and work of the Holy Spirit? Is there any guidance here in our thinking about baptism today?

4 Son and servant. As he was, so are we, his disciples. Which means the more to you—son or servant—in your relationship to God? Have you got the balance right?

——— PRAYERS ———

Now, O Lord, mark their threats, and enable those who serve you to speak your word with all boldness. Stretch out your hand to heal and cause signs and portents to be done through the name of your holy servant Jesus. [1]

> *Almighty God,*
> *whose servant John the Baptist*
> *was wonderfully born to fulfil your purpose*
> *by preparing the way for the advent of your Son:*
> *lead us to repent according to his preaching*
> *and after his example*
> *constantly to speak the truth, boldly rebuke vice,*
> *and patiently suffer for the truth's sake;*
> *through Jesus Christ our Lord.* [2]

Almighty Father, we thank you for our fellowship in the household of faith with all those who have been baptized in your name. Keep us faithful to our baptism, and so make us ready for that day when the whole creation shall be made perfect in your Son, our Saviour Jesus Christ. [3]

> *Lord Jesus Christ,*
> *You have come to us,*
> *You are one with us,*
> *Mary's Son.* [4]

> *Almighty God,*
> *who anointed Jesus at his baptism with the Holy Spirit*
> *and revealed him as your beloved Son:*
> *inspire us, your children,*
> *who are born of water and the Spirit,*

to surrender our lives to your service,
that we may rejoice to be called the sons of God;
through Jesus Christ our Lord.[5]

Temptation

In this chapter, we watch Jesus under attack on a threefold front.

Read **Matthew 4.1–11** (the *order* of the temptations in **Luke 4.1–13** is different).

On the value of desert experience, it would be worthwhile to look at **Galatians 1.15–17**, and at **Amos 1.1** and **7.10–17**.

On the source of Jesus' reply to the tempter, see **Deuteronomy 8.3; 6.16; and 6.13**.

So Jesus was to be the Son-Servant, the Servant-Son. For that he was marked for life—marked possibly for death. Now he could advance from the obscurity of Nazareth to the public ministry of preaching, teaching, and healing. Or could he? Not at once. The implications of such a calling had to be worked out, agonized over, thought and prayed through. There was a testing time to be faced.

It often happens like this. Saul of Tarsus—who was dazzled by the light brighter than the sun, turned round in his tracks, and appointed as servant and witness of Jesus—might have been expected to set off at once on his evangelistic journeys. But he did not. He 'went into Arabia' (Galatians 1.17), there, we cannot doubt, to ponder on the call that had come to him, the meaning of his commission, and the source of the strength he would need in his labours. More things are wrought in the desert than this world dreams of.

——— JESUS IN THE DESERT ———

'For forty days'—that often-used phrase for 'a very long time'— Jesus 'wandered in the wilderness' (Luke 4.1–2). That is a rough phrase and reflects a rough experience. One can get lost in the desert; one can get sun-scorched; one can be chilled to the bone. The desert is an inhospitable place. But Luke says that Jesus was 'led by the Spirit' there. It was a necessary experience, the last and fiercest part of the preparation which tempered the steel of the character of the Servant-Son.

'Led by the Spirit and tempted by the devil', says Luke. The antithesis of these two clauses is suggestive. 'Full of the Holy Spirit', the Spirit who had come upon Jesus in such power at the baptism. 'Led by the Spirit'—propelled on his way. And yet, at the same time, 'tempted by the devil'. It is picture language—how else can spiritual experience be expressed? But it is none the less meaningful for that. We see a man rent, torn, buffeted—and eventually famished.

The desert is a lonely place—no friends there with whom to share one's griefs and perplexities, no warmth of companionship; no one there—except God and the devil! No books to distract the mind— no pictures to hold the attention—no radio or television to amuse. Just God and the devil!

But the desert is also a place of clarity. 'Iona', someone said, 'is a *thin* place'—the eternal impinges on the temporal, the spiritual upon the physical, uninterrupted. There is nothing to spoil the hearing of God's voice, or to impair the vision of the divine. That is how men and women are *made* in the desert. Amos, tending his little flock in the scrubland of Tekoa, is *made* into a man of God who can stand up to the machinations of church and state (**Amos 1.1** and **7.10ff.**). The desert fathers went into desert exile and were *made* into men of God; only then did the people stream out to them for godly counsel and advice, knowing that there their deepest needs would be met.

So it was with Jesus. He needed that long, lonely spell with God, to clarify in his own mind the meaning of his baptismal call to sonship and servanthood; to understand how those two apparent opposites could be held together in a creative tension; to wrestle with the temptation to pursue an easier way; to steel himself for the immense cost which obedience to his call would involve. Only then, with that behind him, would he go, as Luke says he did, 'armed with the power of the Spirit to Galilee' (**Luke 4.14**).

Here, then, we have the clearest clue to the meaning of the three temptations with which Jesus wrestled. He was hammering out what precisely it would mean to be and to act as the Servant-Son. His public ministry was to be short—possibly he sensed that already. Perhaps it would be short and *sharp*—the servant in the servant songs in Isaiah had found that to be the case. Jesus was richly endowed with gifts of the highest order; he must have realized that. How was he to use those gifts? For self-aggrandizement (for, after all, he was a son of the Most High)? Or for service? That was the crux. *Crux* is the Latin word for cross . . .

——— *JESUS' TEMPTATIONS* ———

The bombardment began. It was threefold: the temptation to turn stones into bread; the temptation to cast himself down from the temple parapet; the temptation to do homage to the devil. (The accounts are to be found in the opening verses of **Matthew 4** and **Luke 4**. The order of the temptations varies; we follow Matthew's order in the coming pages.)

—— *Food* **Matthew 4.3–4** ——

The temptation to 'tell these stones to become bread' was twofold. First, Jesus himself 'was famished'—Matthew puts it baldly. Jesus craved for food with a longing unknown to most of us who have never been near the point of starvation. Unless he could eat, and eat soon, there would be no ministry to follow.

Then, too, there were the crowds—he had seen them in the villages, he had seen them in the city of Jerusalem. They were not starving, at least not many of them, but many were undernourished to the point where lassitude set in and there was no energy for creative living. Taxes were high. Wages were low—for some there was the menace of unemployment. The search for adequate nourishment for the family was demanding and exhausting. If the young teacher from the north could present himself as a provider of the means of an easier way of living, life with a measure of comfort to it, what a welcome he would have! He could almost hear the cheers which would greet him.

Food is *good*. Food is *necessary*. Food was needed then and there. So why not use his power to provide it, with the abundance that the Israelites knew when they found the manna in the wilderness? 'Be another Moses, and show yourself as such to the people.' (see **Exodus 16**)

The choice between good and evil, between black and white, is easy. But the choice between good and best is much more difficult, more subtle. Such was the temptation which faced Jesus. It struck at the very heart of the nature of his ministry. What was he to be—the popular dispenser of goods to meet human craving? Or the dispenser of the bread of life, the 'word that comes from the mouth of God' (**Matthew 4.4**)? People can *exist* on bread. But they cannot *live* on that alone. They are made in such a way that they crave for the word of God as a baby craves for its mother's milk.

Jesus would not abandon the best for the good. Others must see to the material and fulfil God's calling to them in that fine way. But for him the choice was clear. The Servant-Son would be the great provider for the *spiritual* hunger of the people—whatever the cost of that provision might be to him.

—— *Sensation* **Matthew 4.5–7** ——

Life was drab for a subject people. The power and the glory belonged to the Roman invader, not to the invaded. The Roman yoke was no joke. The problem of human beastliness to other people nagged like an aching tooth. The bully and the bullied, the wicked and the righteous, justice and retribution—the psalmists wrestled with these problems not always very satisfactorily (can we blame them?). The writer of **Psalm 91** is too facile in the solution he offers—

> You have made the Most High your dwelling-place;
> no disaster will befall you,
> no calamity touch your home.
> For he will charge his angels
> to guard you wherever you go,
> to lift you on their hands
> for fear you strike your foot against a stone.
>
> **(Psalm 91.9–12)**

'The devil can cite Scripture for his purpose'—Shakespeare was right. He tried it on; and the young teacher from Galilee would have none of it. You can't play fast and loose with God, play games with him, strike bargains with him. Life is for real, not for show. The God of the man being tempted was a father-king, longing to live with his people in the intimacy of a father with his children, a king with his subjects. Their long-term welfare was his concern. He was not there to provide a 'sign', a demonstration of dramatic power, a show-piece.

The Servant-Son—should his ministry not be that of a shepherd feeding the sheep, day in day out, guarding and building up the flock, rather than that of a showman entertaining the goats? There would be many who preferred a leader of the latter type, a giver of 'signs', a producer of a show, a display. If the Servant-Son would bend to that, the crowds would follow; they love to have it so. But it would be the denial of everything that he had, during the opening decades of his life, come to see as central to true religion. It could not be.

—— *Power* **Matthew 4.8–10** ——

'All the kingdoms of the world in their glory'—it was a dazzling prospect. Give the young man from Nazareth a horse and a sword. Sweep the Romans into the Mediterranean. Why should not Israel be the means by which the Roman tyranny would be broken, and its Caesar exposed for the hollow man that he was? *There* was a cause good enough to make anyone's heart beat fast. Jesus the Messiah, the man of power, the saviour of his people—perhaps the saviour of the world? People would worship him—everybody loves a success. And look at the perquisites—a throne and the adulation of the nations!

'Out of my sight, Satan! Scripture says, "You shall do homage to the Lord your God and worship him alone".' Power, in Satan's book, means the thrusting aside of God. There is no room for God when the pursuit is for the kingdoms of the world in their glory. Here is stark opposition. It is one or the other—and Jesus sees it with all the clarity of one who has been learning to think of God in terms of fatherhood combined with kingship, and of himself as the Servant-Son. There is an unparalleled peremptoriness about that 'out of my sight, Satan!'

Power—how we love it! If I can make a million before I am twenty-five, all the world lies before me, like an oyster waiting to yield its pearl. A yacht, a Porsche, three houses, and some pretty women or some rich playboys. Money means power.

There can be tyranny in an idea—a political philosophy. Never mind if in its propagation people suffer, are crushed, are heeled into the ground. Never mind if the cost is paid in Siberian prison camps, or Nazi torture chambers, the idea is all. 'All the kingdoms of the world in their glory'.

—— *AFTER TEMPTATION* ——

The bombardment ended. It had involved Jesus in a long engagement, and he was exhausted. 'Then the devil left him,' says Matthew, 'and angels came and attended to his needs'. I wonder what form those angels took—was Mary one of them, with a good hot meal? Luke, in his account, strikes a more sinister note: 'So, having come to the end of all these temptations, the devil departed, *biding his time.*' He must needs lick his wounds, for his defeat had been entire. But it was not for ever—he would be back again. We call this threefold encounter of Jesus with the power of evil '*the* temptation'. But this is a misnomer. The temptation was to go on, throughout the Servant-Son's ministry, into the Garden of Gethsemane, on to the cross . . . While there is life, there is temptation. So he found, and braced himself for a long encounter.

——— QUESTIONS ———

1 Most of us cannot, even if we would like to, get away into the 'desert' for a long period. Yet some provision for aloneness with God is necessary. What, in your experience as a group or as an individual, corresponds in any way with that of Jesus in the wilderness? What plans have you for the future shaping of your life as a disciple?

2 All three temptations had to do with Jesus' scale of values—what matters in the long run? What are the criteria by which you judge your own standards and make your decisions?

3 Jesus had great abilities. Such gifts of God are given to be used, not to be wasted. Paul gives a list of some of them in **Romans 12.6–8**. Has God given you any of these gifts? Has he given you others? Are you using them to the full?

4 To be the son or daughter of a rich father is to have access to power.

To be a servant is to have no power other than what you are.

The Son-Servant worked at getting the balance right. Does he give us, as God's servant-sons and servant-daughters, any direction as to the use of our influence?

—— PRAYERS ——

Lord, we live in a noisy world. We are bombarded with a stream of words.
We talk too much and think too little. Please forgive us.
> *Teach us to be still*
>> *to relax*
>> *to listen*
>> *to imbibe*
>> *to digest.*
> *Save us from the perils of busy-ness*
>> *of hyperactivity*
>> *of the hectic.*
> *Help us to be at peace.*

Almighty God, whose blessed Son was tempted in every way as we are,
yet did not sin:
> *Grant that by your Word and Spirit we may be enabled to triumph*
>> *over every evil,*
> *and to live no longer for ourselves alone, but for him who died*
>> *and rose again for us, Jesus Christ our Lord.*[1]

> *Almighty God,*
> *whose Son Jesus Christ fasted forty days in the wilderness,*
> *and was tempted as we are, yet without sin;*
> *give us grace to discipline ourselves*
>> *in obedience to your Spirit;*
> *and, as you know our weakness,*
> *so may we know your power to save;*
> *through Jesus Christ our Lord.*[2]

TEMPTATION

Lord, we sometimes get caught off guard and temptation leads us into sin.
Remind us that we are frail
that you are strong
that our strength comes from you alone.
In that confidence we are glad. Thank you.

This is our prayer, that our love may grow richer and richer in knowledge and insight of every kind, and may thus bring us the gift of true discrimination. Then on the day of Christ we shall be flawless and without blame.[3]

God, I am so frantic:
somehow I've lost my gentleness
in a flood of ambition,
lost my sense of wonder
in a maze of videos and computers,
lost my integrity
in a shuffle of commercial disguises,
lost my gratitude
in a swarm of criticisms and complaints,
lost my innocence
in a sea of betrayals and compromises.

What can I believe,
except that the touch of your mercy
will ease the anguish of my memory;
that the tug of your spirit
will empower me to help carry now the burdens
I have loaded on the lives of others;
that the example of Jesus
will inspire me to find again my humanity.

THE SERVANT-SON

So, I believe, Lord;
help my unbelief
that I may have courage
to cut free from what I have been
and gamble on what I can be,
and on what you
might laughingly do
with trembling me
for your incredible world.[4]

I AM SILENT . . . AND EXPECTANT

How silently,
how silently
the wondrous gift is given.

I would be silent now,
Lord,
and expectant . . .
that I may receive
the gift I need,
so I may become
the gifts others need.[5]

Suffering Servant

In this chapter, we look at four passages from the book of Isaiah. They speak of a servant of God who was to be called by him, act as his agent, speak for him—and suffer. It is likely that these passages influenced Jesus deeply. They are:

> Isaiah 42.1–9
> Isaiah 49.1–6
> Isaiah 50.4–9
> Isaiah 52.14–53.12

Each one deserves careful study. It could prove worthwhile to delay over each.

We have seen that in the formative years of Jesus' boyhood, adolescence, and young manhood, he was regularly exposed to the influence of the Scriptures (what we call the Old Testament). Saturday by Saturday, in the synagogue, he heard those Scriptures read and expounded. Often those readings gripped him; sometimes his thoughts wandered. Sometimes the sermons held his attention; sometimes they bored him. Sometimes, as on that occasion in the temple when he was twelve, he found the give and take of question and answer between himself and the teachers so enthralling that he lost all sense of time (**Luke 2.41ff.**). Among the Scriptures that he loved most and on which he seems to have meditated longest were the book of Deuteronomy (all his answers to the devil were derived from that book); the Psalms (**Psalm 2**, as we have seen in Chapter 2 was in his mind at his baptism, and he quoted from **Psalm 22.1** and **Psalm 31.5** on the cross) and, surely, the book of the prophet Isaiah. His first sermon was to be based on **Isaiah 61** (see Chapter 5), and there were those passages from **Isaiah** which are called the servant songs.

───── *THE SERVANT SONGS IN ISAIAH* ─────

There are four of them. They are **Isaiah 42.1–9; 49.1–6; 50.4–9;** and **52.14–53.12**. We have already looked at one of them, or, rather, at its beginning (in Chapter 2) and seen that the wording of the voice from heaven was virtually a quotation from **Isaiah 42.1**. The spirit that descended on him there was that of the *servant* as well as that of the son.

Separated though these four passages are from one another in the prophecies which make up the chapters of **Isaiah 40–55**, there is something of a unity about them. Perhaps 'servant songs' is not the best name for them, for there is no suggestion that they have ever been set to music or sung. 'Poems', or perhaps 'prophecies', or 'sketches' might better describe them. To whom do they refer? That is a question which has tantalized readers down the ages.

Luke tells the story (in **Acts 8.26–40**) of the Ethiopian high official who, on returning from a pilgrimage to Jerusalem, was reading, in his carriage, from the last of these passages. Philip, God's agent, joined him, and found himself faced with the very question we are now considering: 'Please tell me . . . who it is that the prophet is speaking about here: himself or someone else?' Philip does not appear to have given a precise answer as to whether it was, as the Ethiopian thought it might have been, a self-portrait of the writer, or whether he had in mind someone else who had suffered for his devotion to God, someone like Jeremiah, for example. Or was it, perhaps, not an individual that was in the prophet's mind, but rather a godly remnant among the Jewish people which for its faithfulness to the God of Israel was the victim of some anti-Semitic outrage? Philip gave no clear answer to these questions. Nor can we with any certainty. The question remains open. But Philip, who presumably knew the passage better than his questioner, found in these verses such 'pointers' to the person of Jesus, such reminders of what Jesus had done through his life and teaching, his passion and crucifixion, that he, Philip, was able 'starting from this passage' to tell 'him the good news of Jesus' (**Acts 8.35**).

The nameless figure of the servant, depicted sometimes puzzlingly, sometimes more clearly, had, as it were, taken flesh and blood in the person of Jesus of Nazareth. Philip was able to say in effect to the Ethiopian: 'This, of which Isaiah wrote, is the one of whom you have just heard in your pilgrimage to Jerusalem, where everyone was talking about the young man from Galilee who had been crucified and, as many were saying, had been raised from death. *This* is *that*!' The official was sufficiently convinced to be baptized and, in his own person, to take the good news of Jesus back to Africa.

In the synagogue, then, and, more rarely, in the temple, Jesus had heard these four passages read. They fascinated him. He went over them in his mind again and again. He had ample opportunity to do so—on the hills where he went to pray; at the carpenter's bench when there was work to do which did not call for much concentration but could be done almost by rote; and, above all, in the long days and longer nights in the desert. That figure—it fascinated him, haunted him, perhaps frightened him. Was it in the mind of his father-God that he, Jesus, might in some way incarnate the figure in those passages, that in his own flesh and blood he might take on the lineaments and the mission of that servant of the Lord? The thought held him—and appalled him. For the servant was a suffering servant. Could it be he? That was part of the agony in the wilderness, the dawning consciousness that there was so much in those passages which fitted in with the concept of his mission as it was forming in his mind. 'Father, I know I am your son. Am I the servant too? Is that the meaning of sonship? Father, is it I?'

We must look at those passages one by one.

——— Isaiah 42.1–9 ———

'He will not shout or raise his voice, or make himself heard in the street' (v. 2). There is no need to do that. Noisy shouting can be left to other orators, with their superficial panaceas for world needs. There is about the servant of the Lord a quiet authority which is self-authenticating. No thrusting of himself and his credentials here! Indeed, he does not seem to be concerned about himself at all—his concern is about others. In his mind's eye he sees a crushed reed, to all intents and purposes useless—it has got broken through nature's or man's rough handling. Most people would snap it off and throw it away. Not so the servant. Suppose it could be mended, brought back to usefulness: there is life in it yet . . .? Or again he sees a smouldering wick; it had been made to give light, and now all that it emits is a stench. Snuff it out—it's a nuisance. Not so the servant. Suppose it could be coaxed back to life and light, re-established in its place of honour in the household? Why not? The servant's God was the God of hope (**Romans 15.13**). And the carpenter of Nazareth was well-practised in mending broken things.

There is infinite tenderness here and patience beyond all telling. There is steel as well—'He will never falter or be crushed' (**Isaiah 42.4**). Though all the world is against him, he will go on, with an endurance rooted in his faith in the God of justice whom the servant represents. There is nothing sloppy or sentimental about the servant's tenderness. He has a concern for justice which enlarges his vision and his mission—he looks out to 'the nations' (**Isaiah 42.1**), to 'coasts and islands' which 'await his teaching' (**Isaiah 42.4**).

His sense of call is crystal-clear. 'I the Lord have called you . . . taken you by the hand . . . formed you . . . destined you' (**Isaiah 42.6**). This is the stuff of which prophets are made—'Whom shall I send? Who will go for us?' The questions were a summons to young Isaiah, and the only answer he could give was: 'Here am I! Send me' (**Isaiah 6.9**). It was so with Jeremiah, young, shy, diffident. 'Before I formed you in the womb I chose you . . . I consecrated you . . . I appointed you . . .' **(Jeremiah 1.5)**. That call brooks no refusal. Church and State might combine against Amos—'Seer, go away! Off with you to Judah! Earn your living and do your prophesying there . . . this is a royal shrine.' What answer can a crude country man give to such threatening? 'I was no prophet—nor was I a prophet's son . . . But the Lord took me . . . it was the Lord who said to me "Go and prophesy . . ."' **(Amos 7.10ff.)**.

There is steel here. In the servant's case, that steel derives its strength from two sources—*first*, that the God who calls him is the God of infinite power (he 'fashioned the earth'), the source of life and growth, ('giving breath to its people and life to those who walk in it'—**Isaiah 42.5**) and *second*, that the purpose of his call is spelt out with clarity. The servant knows his destiny and his aim. It is 'to be a lamp for nations, to open eyes that are blind, to bring captives out of prison . . .' **(Isaiah 42.6–7)**. No vague philosophy is envisaged here. There are people to be reached, prisoners to be released.

The prophet's God is no new God. 'I am the Lord' **(Isaiah 42.8)**, the same Lord who revealed his name to Moses at the burning bush **(Exodus 3.13ff.)**, the 'I am' (or, perhaps more significantly, the 'I will be'). No man-made god like the gods of the surrounding peoples, but a God jealous for his honour and his holiness.

No new God—but nevertheless a God whose eyes are always open to the future, whose revelation has no closure date to it. 'The earlier prophecies have come to pass, and now I declare new things . . . I announce them to you.' **(Isaiah 42.9)** The servant is in on the councils of the Most High, sharing his mind, declaring his purpose. The declaration is of the very essence of his servanthood. He would not be a servant if he were unfaithful in announcing the ancient name of his God ('I am the Lord') and the ever-new, ever-developing outworking of his plan for mankind.

——— Isaiah 49.1–6 ———

The servant's mission is not limited to his own people. As in the first passage his eye is on 'the nations' and the 'coasts and islands' **(Isaiah 42.1, 4)**, so here 'coasts and islands, peoples far distant' come within the range of his mission. His sense of call is as clear here as it was in **Isaiah 42**—he has been 'named . . . from my mother's womb' (**Isaiah 49.1**).

How is his mission to be fulfilled? He envisages it in terms of battle. There is a fight to be fought—a sword will be called for, an arrow and a quiver (**Isaiah 49.2**). Is he then going to be a warrior as people conceive of warriors, his strength consisting in violence and arms? Not at all. His *tongue* is his sword and he himself is the arrow—indeed God has 'made' him into that (**Isaiah 49.2**). Of that we shall hear more when we come to the third passage (**Isaiah 50.4**).

The servant allows us to share in the intimacy of his call and his spiritual experience. God had spoken to him—he was to be one through whom God's glory would be seen (**Isaiah 49.3**). But he was not immune from those temptations which assail all God's messengers, not least that of depression (**Isaiah 49.4**).

When things were at their darkest in World War II, Churchill quoted the words of the poet A. H. Clough:

> Say not, the struggle naught availeth,
> The labour and the wounds are vain,
> The enemy faints not, nor faileth,
> And as things have been they remain. . . .
>
> For while the tired waves, vainly breaking,
> Seem here no painful inch to gain,
> Far back, through creeks and inlets making,
> Comes silent, flooding in, the main.
>
> And not by eastern windows only,
> When daylight comes, comes in the light,
> In front, the sun climbs slow, how slowly,
> But westward, look, the land is bright.

The 'west' meant for Churchill American aid. The servant rallies with a stronger hope than that of Clough or Churchill. Though the odds against him seem overwhelming, he stays himself on God—'My cause is with the Lord and my reward with my God.' (**Isaiah 49.4**, author's italics)

He looks back to that original call and to the terms of his commission as he then understood it. His mission was to *Israel*—'to bring Jacob back to' the God they had forsaken, 'that Israel should be gathered to him' (**Isaiah 49.5**). But *now* the horizons are broader, no longer are they limited to Israel. He, the servant, is to be 'a light to the *nations*, so that my salvation may reach earth's farthest bounds' (**Isaiah 49.6**, author's italics).

There is a universality to the servant's message which no nationalism must narrow or thwart.

> There's a wideness in God's mercy
> like the wideness of the sea.

The servant is to be an instrument in the fulfilling of a vision outlined in an earlier chapter when

> many peoples will go and say,
> 'Let us go up to the mountain of the Lord,
> to the house of the God of Jacob,
> that he may teach us his ways
> and that we may walk in his paths.'
> For instruction comes from Zion,
> and the word of the Lord from Jerusalem. (**Isaiah 2.3**)

Jerusalem with its lofty monotheism and high ethic will be a centre of light for all who come to her, from whatever distance they come, and the servant will forward the cause of their enlightenment and be the instrument of their salvation.*

――― **Isaiah 50.4–9** ―――

The servant in the second passage had touched on the subject of his tongue being the sword and himself the arrow in the battle to which God had committed him (**Isaiah 49.2**). Here in the third passage

---

*Most commentators hold that the second song ends here at **Isaiah 49.6**. The succeeding verses are in a different rhythm and, unlike **Isaiah 49.1–6**, are represented as a speech of the Lord and not of the servant.

the theme is renewed and developed. Indeed, it is the subject matter of the opening two verses (4 and 5). Speaking and hearing, listening and the saying of a timely word—this is how the servant describes his task. He is a man under instruction (**Isaiah 50.4**), his hearing sharpened, his ears opened, his will obedient, ready to fulfil his role. By inference, we see God as the great instructor, the alerter ('he made my hearing sharp'), the stimulator of mind and conscience— the kind of activity of which the author of the fourth Gospel was to speak when he referred to the Holy Spirit as *paraclete* (**John 14–16**). 'Every morning' the Lord is at his sharpening work, when the servant was fresh and open, and the world was still. The servant is too wise to rush into battle unprepared, to speak before he has listened, to run on the mission without being sure what the mission is about and what he has to say. He must undergo instruction—and not only at the beginning of his mission but 'every morning'. Yesterday's manna will not do for today. His hearing apparatus must be kept in good repair, else his sword will be blunt and his speaking so much hot air. His *will* must be at the ready ('I did not disobey or turn back . . .' **Isaiah 50.5**)

He might have turned back, for he was soon to learn that being a spokesman of God involved suffering. The 'cost of discipleship' is heavy, as Dietrich Bonhoeffer knew when he wrote a book with that title and when he went to martyrdom under Hitler's dreadful régime. 'I offered my back to the lash . . . I did not hide my face from insult and spitting.' (**Isaiah 50.6**)

The servant touches briefly on this matter of suffering in this passage. He is to develop it at length and in depth in the last of the four passages.

He is the subject of insults (**Isaiah 50.7**). He does not describe their nature here, but it takes little imagination to guess what they were like. His very character was a rebuke to his opponents—it hurt their consciences. His stress on silent listening morning by morning seemed nonsense to the members of an activist society. Why this emphasis on *words*? 'We prefer the big battalions!' The opposition has been repeated in a thousand forms over the millennia, and it hurts no less today for having been used so often before.

We mentioned the steel of the servant's character (See **Isaiah 42.4**). Here he speaks of setting 'my face like a flint' (**Isaiah 50.7**).

When it comes to judgement day, he has no fears. He can throw out an invitation to confrontation. There is a hint of taunting in the questions: 'Who dare argue against me? . . . Who will dispute my cause?' (**Isaiah 50.8**) He is ready to take his opponents on—'Let us confront one another . . . Let him come forward.' How can this be? Is it cockiness on the part of the servant? On the contrary, it is naked godliness—'The Lord God is my helper.' (**Isaiah 50.9**) 'All my hope on God is founded.' Right will ultimately prevail. The forces of evil have within them the seeds of decay. God has not abdicated. He and he alone is the source of the servant's confidence.

——— Isaiah 52.14–53.12 ———

This, the longest of the passages, opens with a note of strong surprise. The figure of the servant, here described in considerable detail, is the last that we should expect in one who is to accomplish God's work. Surely we should look for a fine figure of a man, mounted perhaps on a charger, surrounded with all the panoply of power. 'Who could have believed what we have heard? To whom has the power of the Lord been revealed?' (**Isaiah 53.1**) Here is depicted a man so disfigured as to be almost unrecognizable, and people's minds boggle as they behold him (**Isaiah 52.14–15**). Here is no Adonis, no incarnation of beauty. If you want an analogy from nature, here is no luxuriant plant growing up in succulent soil, but 'a young plant whose roots are in parched ground' (**Isaiah 53.2**); we all know what such plants look like and what their ultimate fate is.

We noted how, in the third passage, the servant briefly mentioned the suffering which obedience to his mission entailed (**Isaiah 50.6**). In this, the fourth passage, the theme is enlarged and expounded—indeed, the major part of the chapter is given over to it. The colours of the picture are not always clearly defined—they merge in a mystery. But what else should we expect when the theme is suffering, suffering undeserved, suffering unresented, suffering vicarious? Suffering always is a mystery. It can often lead to bitterness. There is none of that here.

Accepted, if not fully understood, there is no railing against God on the part of the servant as he suffers. The great figures of the Old Testament cry out to God and often against God, charging him with being asleep. The psalmists, for example, dare to say: 'Rouse yourself, Lord; why do you sleep? Awake! Do not reject us for ever. Why do you hide your face?' (**Psalm 44.23–24**). Or again:

> Will the Lord always reject me
> and never again show favour?
> Has his love now failed utterly?
> Will his promise never be fulfilled?
> Has God forgotten to be gracious?
> Has he in anger withheld his compassion?
> 'Has his right hand grown weak?' I said.
> 'Has the right hand of the Most High changed?'
> (**Psalm 77.7–10**)

The prophets, too, break out in protest. Honest Jeremiah looks up to God and says: 'You have duped me, Lord, and I have been your dupe; you have outwitted me and prevailed. All the day long I have been made a laughing-stock; everyone ridicules me.' (**Jeremiah 20.7**) The book of Job is one long cry—I had almost said 'scream'—about unmerited pain. But here in **Isaiah 53** is another kind of suffering. The servant suffers in silence—twice in one verse it is said that 'he did not open his mouth.' (**Isaiah 53.7**) He takes the maltreatment, the arrest and sentence, the fate assigned to him, the deprivation of life, death itself (**Isaiah 53.7–8**), into his own person, not negatively but positively and redemptively. Something wonderfully creative is to be seen here—it is 'for us', and by his wounds we are healed (**Isaiah 53.5**). Vicarious suffering has immense restorative power.

In this strange figure, we begin to see the cross of Christ, and the symbol of shame becomes the very centre of our hope. We begin to see why John Bunyan made Christian cry out as he saw the cross on the hill:

> Blest cross!   blest sepulchre!
> Blest rather be the man who there was crucified for me!

In this profound passage there is no blurring of the fact of human sin. 'Our pain—our transgressions—our iniquities—our straying . . .' it is all there. Every one of us is caught up in that unholy bundle of life and consequent death. But divine action through the suffering servant takes place and 'the chastisement he bore restored us to health and by his wounds we are healed'. (Isaiah 53.5) No cheap grace here, but costly deliverance. Here is no ordinary martyrdom. This is not just one more human tragedy. 'God was in Christ reconciling the world to himself.' (2 Corinthians 5.19)

There is a notable change in the tone of the latter part of this servant song passage. The opening half (Isaiah 52.14–53.9) deals with the stern realities of human sin and error, and with the cost of forgiveness. There is no trivialization, no letting off the hook. But in the second half, the minor tone gives way to the major. The sun begins to shine. The suffering of the servant is not in vain—'In his hand the Lord's purpose will prosper. By his humiliation my servant will justify many', and the servant himself will 'see light and be satisfied' (Isaiah 53.10–11).*

——— *JESUS THE SERVANT* ———

These, then, were the four passages on which Jesus pondered. Gradually the figure emerged in his mind—a figure with an authority which was self-authenticating; a figure infinitely gentle in his handling of broken things and yet with an element of steel in his endurance; a figure who conceived of his mission in world terms; a warrior with words as his weapons and with God as his confidence; a servant who was both learner and teacher; the subject of insults, despised and rejected of men, chosen of God to bring forgiveness and healing to humankind.

Meditating on this figure—as Jesus strode over the hills, worked at the carpenter's bench, prayed with his father God—it seemed to him to fit in with what his mother had taught him ('I am the Lord's servant; may it be as you have said'); with what the voice from heaven had said at his baptism when the Spirit of servanthood came upon the son; with what had emerged as the central issue of the threefold temptation in the wilderness—his way was not to be the

---

*The pattern of this passage is that also of **Psalm 22**, where the opening stanzas are in the minor key (**Psalm 22.1–21**) and the closing ones in the major (**Psalm 22.22–31**).

way of power and force but the way of 'weakness', of love and self-giving and therefore of suffering. It was all of a piece. There was a unity about the picture that was emerging from those long years of waiting. God had been at work in the heart and mind of that developing young man. The Servant-Son was ready to emerge into the glare of public ministry.

The quartet of passages from Isaiah proved to be seminal in the thinking of Jesus—perhaps more definitive of the nature of his imminent ministry than any other passage in the Scriptures.

The temptation in the wilderness now behind him, the sermon at Nazareth lay immediately ahead. That was to clinch what had been forming in his mind.

—— *QUESTIONS* ——

1 Peter, in his first letter (**1 Peter 2.19–25**), clearly had in mind the last of the servant-songs of Isaiah (**Isaiah 52.14–53.12**). What moral lessons does he draw from his meditation?

2 The influence of his Bible on Jesus seems to have been profound. The same Spirit who taught him is at hand to teach us. What opportunities do we give him to do so?

3 Tenderness and strength; gentleness and steel combine in Isaiah's picture of the servant. Can you think of anyone you have known in whom these contrasting qualities meet?

4 'You are not what you think you are. But what you think, you are.' In other words, right thinking leads to right character. Paul speaks of being 'transformed by the renewal of your minds' (**Romans 12.2**). That does not mean that, if we are to know God and discover his will, we must all be clever. What *does* it mean?

 *PRAYERS*

Father of mankind,
who gave your only-begotten Son
to take upon himself the form of a servant
and to be obedient even to death on a cross:
give us the same mind that was in Christ Jesus
that, sharing his humility,
we may come to be with him in his glory;
who is alive and reigns with you and the Holy Spirit,
one God, now and for ever.[1]

Father, we bring to you the needs of those whose lives are shadowed by
suffering, praying especially for those
      whose sickness has no cure,
      whose sadness finds no comfort,
      and whose loneliness can never be filled.
   Bind up their wounds, O Lord,
   and lift their hearts to you,
as now in silence we remember them in Jesus' name.[3]

Have compassion, O Lord, on those who are depressed and cast down in
spirit.
   Let your light shine upon their darkness.
   Rekindle in them the lamp of hope.
   Give them the assurance of your unchanging love and unfailing
      companionship;
   and so give them courage to face life bravely,
   in the name and strength of Jesus Christ our Saviour.[4]

O Master, in whose life I see
All that I long but fail to be,
Let thy clear light for ever shine
To shame and guide this life of mine.

Though what I dream and what I do
In my poor days are always two,
Help me, oppressed by things undone,
O thou, whose deeds and dreams were one.[5]

Blessed Lord,
who caused all holy Scriptures
    to be written for our learning:
help us so to hear them,
            to read,
                mark,
                learn,
                and inwardly digest them
that, through patience, and the comfort
    of your holy word,
we may embrace and for ever hold fast
    the hope of everlasting life,
which you have given us in our Saviour Jesus Christ.[2]

We pray for those who translate the Scriptures into other languages
                who disseminate them throughout the world
                who comment on and expound them
                who read them in public worship
                who study them at home;
    that the Holy Spirit will guide them into all truth.

First Sermon

In this chapter, we see Jesus at work, preaching in the synagogue of his home town. We note the effect of the sermon on his audience.

The passages to study are **Luke 4.16–30** and **Isaiah 61.1–3** on which Jesus based his sermon.

Luke is a skilled storyteller. No wonder that tradition has depicted him as an artist with palette and paints in his hands. Certainly he is an artist with words. Nowhere is this seen better than in his story of Jesus preaching his first sermon. To that story we now turn. It is in **Luke 4.16–30**.

The scene is Nazareth, the town where Jesus had been brought up. He knew that synagogue well, for he had worshipped there week after week since he was a tot. Now, as a mature young man of about thirty, he stands up to read the lesson—the custom was to *stand* to read the Scriptures, to *sit* to expound them. Was the passage the lection appointed for the day? Or did he choose it himself? We do not know. It matters little. 'He opened the scroll'—much more difficult than opening a modern book with page numbers but 'he found the passage . . .'. Now he was well away—'The Spirit of the Lord is upon me', he read, 'because he has anointed me.' It was wonderfully apposite. That was exactly what had happened to him down at the river Jordan. The Spirit of the Lord had come upon him like a dove, the gentle Spirit of Servant-Sonship. He could never forget that day. It was definitive for his whole mission. In *that* spirit he would go to his work. He longed to get going, because he loved the people and wanted to minister to them.

Isaiah (Jesus was reading from the prophecy, **Isaiah 61**) could not have spelled out Jesus' mission better if he had tried:

> He has sent me to announce good news to the poor,
> to proclaim release for prisoners
> and recovery of sight for the blind;
> to let the broken victims go free,
> to proclaim the year of the Lord's favour. (**Luke 4.18–19**)

There was a light in the reader's eye, the light that can only come from a clear sense of mission, of divine call—'He has sent me.' God's finger had touched him. His heart was full of compassion—for the poor, the prisoners, the blind, the broken . . . (compare **Isaiah 42.7**). How wonderful to be God's man, God's apostle to them! 'Today, in your hearing, this text has come true.' (**Luke 4.21**)

If Jesus was happy with his text, the people were happy with their preacher. Many of them had known him all his life. They had watched him grow up, seen him develop. Today he was the same—and yet different. He was a man with a mission, a divine mission. This sermon was unlike anything they had heard before. 'They were astonished that words of such grace should fall from his lips.' (Luke 4.22) This was *real* religion. If this was true, then they would embrace it and be embraced by it. This was *real* preaching. They sensed a lifting of their spirits, as if a load were being taken from their shoulders. 'Good news', Isaiah had said. 'Good news', Jesus read out. An 'announcement', a 'proclamation' (Luke 4.18), not a demand or another load to crush their consciences. They knew the passage well enough to note the point where Jesus stopped reading and sat down. Isaiah had said 'a day of the vengeance of our God' (Isaiah 61.2). Jesus had omitted that—the day of wrath was not yet. He announced a day of *grace*—'The year of the Lord's favour' (Luke 4.19). The young man who read those words from Isaiah seemed himself to be an embodiment of God's grace. There was about him a graciousness which was beautiful—almost yearning, infinitely caring.

We must pause for a moment on the words 'the year of the Lord's favour', with which Jesus closed the quotation from Isaiah 61.2. The 'coming out' of Jesus from the comparative hiddenness of Galilee into the full glare of his public ministry was accurately timed by the God who never gets his timing wrong. It was 'the year which God has graciously appointed in order to show his salvation', the year of jubilee, the year of liberation.* God's clock had struck, and men and women must hear its chime. God's kingdom, his reign, was being inaugurated in a way people had never seen before.

'The kingdom of God' is an oft-recurring expression in the teaching of Jesus, and his use of the phrase is sometimes tantalizingly difficult. Clearly, it was to him a present reality. In his own person its arrival could be seen, as people's enemies were conquered (demons were cast out). In that conquest, the very finger of God was at work, operating among the crowds (Luke 11.20). The 'finger of God'—what a daring phrase! The reign of God was *there*, for all to see; only the spiritually blind could miss it. The poor, the prisoners, the blind,

---

*See Howard Marshall, in his *Commentary on the Gospel of Luke*, The Paternoster Press, 1978, p. 184.

the broken, found their needs met in the arrival of the man from Nazareth.

But the phrase 'the reign (or kingdom) of God' has a future content to it. Jesus bade his disciples to pray 'your kingdom come'. For if it is true that its arrival was manifested in the coming of Christ—and the evidences for that were on all hands as he did his teaching, preaching, and healing work—the consummation of that kingdom lay ahead. That is why there has to be a chapter in this book (Chapter 8) entitled 'Servant-Son Church', for the reign of God inaugurated by the Servant-Son has to be pursued by his followers in every generation. That pursuit is beset by difficulties, for the powers of darkness are strong. But wherever a poor man is enriched, a prisoner is set free, wherever a blind woman has her eyes opened, or a broken woman has her fetters loosed, there the reign of God is advanced. Wherever society is made more healthy, its legislation made more righteous, its government made more upright, there the reign of God is advanced. The church of God is the nucleus of the kingdom, the spearhead of its advance; its members exist for that very purpose. But often that reign comes through men and women who do not acknowledge the Servant-Son or who have never heard of him or come under his sway. For the kingdom is a wider concept than that of the church, and to equate the one with the other is to go astray. Wherever truth, goodness, or beauty gain ground, there is a victory for the reign of God. It is significant that the prayer 'your kingdom come' stands next to 'your will be done'.

We shall see (for example, in Chapter 6) that Jesus spoke of God mainly in terms of 'father' and 'king'. A father seeks a family where love prevails, love for him, mutual love among its members, love reaching out to the world. A king seeks citizens whose loyalty leads to the doing of his righteous will, and peace reigns in justice and equity. The kingdom of God meant to Jesus paternal government.

The choice of this passage from **Isaiah 61** as the text for the first sermon of Jesus' public ministry was not haphazard. It was a declaration of intent. It was a hoisting of his flag, so that all could see the nature of the ministry on which he was embarking. It was a nailing of his colours to the mast. It was his programme in a nutshell—to go to the poor, the prisoners, the blind, the broken. It was liberation. It was life. The son was to be the servant, not wielding the sword of power, but going the way of love, his weapons a bowl for washing their feet and a cross for bearing their sins.

All four Gospels spell out how Jesus fulfilled the mission which he outlined in his first sermon. He had his contacts with the well-to-do—among his followers who provided for him and his disciples out of their own resources was Joanna, wife of Chuza, a steward of Herod's (**Luke 8.3**); and he addressed himself to the needs of a rich ruler (**Luke 18.18–27**). But it seems that his *main* energies were devoted to the broken victims of a harsh society. We may take very literally the words of his text. But, of course, the words have a deeper meaning. 'The prisoners' were not only those who languished in Herod's gaols; they were the prisoners of habits which they could not control, desires that overmastered them. The 'blind' were not only those who suffered from lack of physical sight. They were people by whom the beauty of God had never been seen and for whom the glory of God was a meaningless term. The 'broken victims' were not only those whom a rough society had cast up like driftwood on the shore and left untended. They were the men and women whose relationships with God, with their fellows, and with themselves were so strained that they had snapped—victims of physical, nervous, or mental breakdown. Such victims were to be found in all strata of society in Jesus' day: they are today—on the luxury yacht and in the city slum, all alike in a oneness of need. *They* were the people to whom the Servant-Son was sent, sent to heal and to save.

The immediate response to the reading of the passage from **Isaiah 61** was what we might have expected; there was something about the young man who read it which appealed to his hearers. But the sequel to that first response was astonishing (**Luke 4.23–30**). It was as if the sun had gone in and the thunderclouds were banking up. Jesus knew what was in people; and he knew his Jewish history. He knew how often, in times gone by, God had sent his messengers, and they themselves and the messages they brought had been rejected by the people. As he expounded his theme of God's message and of God's grace coming to people beyond the borders of the Jewish nation, the smile on the faces of the congregation turned from pleasure to pain, to perplexity, to resistance, even to hatred. Jesus sketched the story of Elijah (**1 Kings 17**) who was rejected by his own people and, on his rejection, was sent to a widow living outside the territory of the promised land. He touched on the story of Elisha (2 Kings 5.1–19) whose ministry, opposed within Israel, reached out to Naaman, a Syrian 'outsider'. Did God care for Gentiles as he cared for his 'own people', the Jews? Did race matter not one whit to him? If the heart was right, was the colour of the skin irrelevant? Was the mission of this young man preaching to them in the synagogue that day to be on *those* lines—a mission with a universal outreach? Surely, Israel was privileged above all the rest. This would not do. The thunderclouds broke. His words 'roused the whole congregation to fury; they leapt up, drove him out of the town, and took him to the brow of the hill on which it was built, meaning to hurl him over the edge' (Luke 4.28–29). It was only something about him, a kind of holiness and majesty, which saved him from the violence of their hands. Vengeance, the crowd said, must wait for another day. His time will come. We will get him.

It was an ugly scene. Purity makes people look shabby. Crowds are fickle, their reactions unpredictable. Jesus, with his clarity of vision, saw that day what his mission, if faithfully fulfilled, might lead him to. Love and service often lead to suffering, sometimes even to a cross . . .

—— QUESTIONS ——

1 When the writer of the letter to the Ephesians was outlining God's gifts to his church, he included 'some to be . . . prophets' (**Ephesians 4.11**). How do you define 'prophet'? It might help to identify two Old Testament prophets, two New Testament ones, two present-day world figures, and two whom you know.

2 'The church should not allow itself to get mixed up in politics.' The statement is often made. How does this passage throw light on it?

3 Has the story of **Luke 4.16–30** anything to teach us about race relationships? If so, what might be the implications of this teaching in present-day Europe, in this country, in your town, in your street?

4 We all have our hang-ups—hang-ups on race
            gender
            social relations, and so
            on.
Could the Nazareth preacher shed light on, or even resolve, your particular one?

—— PRAYERS ——

From moral weakness of spirit, from timidity, from fear of other people and dread of responsibility, strengthen us to speak the truth with the strength that can yet speak in love and self-control; and alike from the weakness of hasty violence and the weakness of moral cowardice, save us and help us, we humbly beseech thee, O Lord.[1]

We pray for the courage to speak the truth
for the strength to respond to truth
for grace to respect the views of others
for love to embrace those from whom we differ.
We pray for those who preach, that
the love of God may be in their hearts
words of grace may fall from their lips
the light of hope may shine in their eyes.

Almighty God,
Who gave to your apostles
grace truly to believe and to preach your word:
grant that your church
may love that word which they believed
and may faithfully preach and receive the same;
through Jesus Christ our Lord.

A prayer for preacher and listener:
Lord, may I speak
and may we hear
the word of God,
that we may be able to discern your will
and to know what is good, acceptable and perfect.

6

Minister of Health

In this chapter, we consider the main purpose of the ministry of Jesus: to lead men and women to 'salvation', to wholeness of being, to holiness.

How he set about it is sketched in **Matthew 4.23–25** and **9.35–36**.

The negative aim of Jesus' work was to do battle against ignorance, sin, and disease (pp. 60–65).

The positive aim was to bring about 'peace' (pp. 65–72).

To fulfil his purpose, Jesus taught, preached, healed. These activities were not separate entities—they flowed into each other.

We glance at Jesus as teacher   (pp. 61–62)
                     as preacher (pp. 63–64)
                     as healer   (pp. 64–65)

We give five instances of Jesus' healing work. (The reference for each is given on pp. 66–71). Each could serve as the basis for a separate study session.

People used to bring their broken things to the carpenter's shop at Nazareth—a table that would not stand straight, a bench that creaked, a yoke that irked the oxen's necks—and Joseph and his young assistant would mend them. They were good at that. We may hazard a guess that they made a bit of a reputation for themselves for work well done.

There was a certain continuity between the work done during the long years which Jesus spent in the shop and the work on which he was now embarking in his public ministry. That much shorter period of his life was now to be given wholly to *mending the broken*—only now it was persons rather than tables or benches or yokes. Now he was to labour with more intractable material—'broken victims' as Isaiah had put it in the text on which Jesus had based his first sermon. Broken personalities, broken hearts, these were to be his concern as he turned his back on the shop and gave himself to the threefold task of preaching, teaching, and healing.

There was another and deeper continuity which we should notice. John records Jesus as saying: 'My Father continues to work, and I must work too' (John 5.17). The idea of God as the great worker is central to many strands of Old Testament teaching. Jesus must have delighted in thinking of God in those terms—God not only as the creator when things first came to be but also as the one who continues to work with his creation, making all things new, venturing out into the unknown. He had it in mind that Israel would co-operate with him in that continuing creation and re-creation, but again and again that nation failed to glimpse the vision and to give practical expression to it. Now Jesus, in his own person, picks up the task. 'For me it is meat and drink to do the will of him who sent me until I have finished his work.' (John 4.34) 'Until . . .'; he was at last to cry from the cross: 'It is accomplished!' (John 19.30) 'Then', and only then, did he 'bow his head and give up his spirit'. He was to be the spearhead of God's redeeming, re-creative purpose for his world.

As Jesus got to work, he noticed that the broken people found their way to him. He liked it like that, though the pressure of numbers often made it difficult for him. He liked it like that because he saw himself as a shepherd, and a shepherd spends time on a torn lamb or a sheep with a broken limb out of all proportion to the time he spends on the healthy ones. 'It is not the healthy who need a doctor, but the sick; I did not come to call the virtuous, but sinners', he said (**Mark 2.17**). People came to him broken and he healed them, or set them on the road to health. It did not always happen like that, by any means, for the material was often resistant to change. But often there was healing, and Jesus rejoiced, and so did the angels (**Luke 15.10**).

When doctors handle sick patients, they have two main aims in view. The first is a *negative* one: to destroy all the forces which are attacking the patient's body or mind. The second is a *positive* one: to seek to set in motion a process by which the patient may become a whole man or woman, a rounded personality, resistant to attack, and open to development.

These were the aims of Jesus in his dealings with people. We must consider each in turn:

——— THE NEGATIVE AIM ———

The *negative* aim is *to destroy the forces which attack the patient*. The Bible takes for granted the fact that something has gone wrong with humankind. It never seeks to avoid that truth. The picture stories in the opening chapters of Genesis seek to emphasize it: Adam and Eve live in innocence, in happy relationship with God and with one another. Then things go wrong. They have to hide from God. God has to go searching for them—'Adam, where are you?' (**Genesis 3.9**) The stories set the scene which is developed in all the ensuing books in the Old Testament library. Then comes the announcement to Joseph that Mary 'will bear a son; and you shall give him the name Jesus, for he will save his people from their sins' (**Matthew 1.21**). A rescue operation, destructive of the opposing forces, is to take place; a deliverer is about to appear. 'Jesus' is the Greek form of the Hebrew word 'Joshua', and Joshua has gone down in history as the great liberator of the Israelite nation, the one who was to see his people *out* of the bondage of Egypt *into* the freedom of the promised land. (See **Joshua 1** for the beginning of the story). The opposition would be long and the fight hard, but there would be victory at the end.

Jesus took for granted the radical sickness of men and women. He did not argue whence this sickness came, or produce a thesis on its cure. The thing was there, and he was to tackle it—in his day-to-day ministry, and in his own person. People were to say of him that he reminded them of Isaiah's picture of the servant: 'He took our illnesses from us and carried away our diseases.' (**Matthew 8.17**, referring back to **Isaiah 53.4**)

It seems clear that Jesus saw three main forces at work in spoiling God's plan for his creatures, three enemies against which he must go into battle. They were ignorance, sin, and disease. Matthew, in an admirable summary of the main activities of Jesus' mission, summed them up as 'teaching, proclaiming the good news, and healing' (**Matthew 4.23** and **9.35**). These were his weapons:

> As he *taught*, he pushed back the tide of *ignorance*.
> As he *preached*, he pushed back the tide of *sin*.
> As he *healed*, he pushed back the tide of *sickness and disease*.

In doing so, he worked out the meaning of his name Jesus: Saviour, Deliverer—and people marvelled. God had been visiting and redeeming his people; a greater than Joshua was here!

Jesus the Teacher—Let us watch him at his teaching. There were teachers in plenty in Israel when Jesus went to work. Rabbis abounded. But when this young man stood up to teach, his hearers realized that they were seeing and hearing something new. They were surprised and thrilled. Mark, in the opening chapter of his Gospel, captures something of their astonishment—'The people were amazed at his teaching, for, unlike the scribes, he taught with a note of authority.' (**Mark 1.22**) They exclaimed: 'What is this? A new kind of teaching! He speaks with authority . . .' (**Mark 1.27**) There was a freshness about it which they had not encountered before—those parables, so earthy in their illustrations, were heavenly! Jesus could be radical, sweeping away the peripheral things that mattered little, and piercing to the heart of the matter—as when with one stroke he did away with the relevance of the Jewish food-laws and insisted that what entered into a man's stomach mattered little, what proceeded from his heart mattered much (**Mark 7.14–23**). 'You have heard that our forefathers were told . . . but what I tell you is this . . .' (**Matthew 5.21–22, 27–28, 31–32, 33–34, 38–39, 43–44**) How dare he teach like this? But just when they were about to dismiss him and his teaching, they thought again: whence this *authority*? There was that about the young teacher which was self-authenticating; was it the authority of holiness? No wonder that the crowds hung on his words—'No one ever spoke as this man speaks' they said (**John 7.46**). They listened and watched him at work till the sun went down; they even forgot their physical hunger (**Matthew 14.13–21**). *This* was the bread of life!

Jesus never talked down at them. He would often tell a story and not draw out the moral. That was *their* job. He was there to alert mind and conscience, to use stories as a way to the heart, to stir imagination. 'What do *you* think?' he would say; 'How does it seem to *you*?' (**Matthew 18.12; 21.28**, author's italics) The old hard ground of their minds would be softened by the rain of his teaching, the seed could be sown, and the plant would grow. It was all so refreshing, new, enlivening.

This was no gloomy teacher. The very reverse was the case. It would seem that the two cries of Jesus which the evangelists remembered best were: 'Don't be scared', and 'Take heart' or, as we should say, 'Cheer up'. The opening verses of the sermon on the mount (the beatitudes) are really a description of the essentially happy man or woman—the disciple who has learned to sit loose to what most people think are the things which matter, and is learning the secrets that belong to the children of God's reign. It may surprise a casual reader of that sermon (**Matthew 5–7**) to notice how strongly Jesus condemns worry (**Matthew 6.25ff.**). Why? Because worrying shows that the worrier has forgotten that there is a father who cares about his children. That is a profound truth: worry is the opposite of faith. Faith is what happens when a child, in the darkness of the night, slips his hand into his father's. There was nothing facile about those cries: 'Don't be scared', 'Cheer up.' They were the expression of the teacher's deep experience of God. God has not abdicated. He still reigns.

Ignorance is darkness, and darkness is sinister. Jesus by his teaching attacked that enemy and, as he did so, the darkness began to disperse. 'The light shines in the darkness, and the darkness has never mastered it.' (**John 1.5**)

Jesus the Preacher—Let us watch him at his preaching. It is not possible to draw a steady dividing line between teaching and preaching. Preaching which does not contain an ingredient of teaching is not worth much. Every sermon presents the preacher with an opportunity to teach, to show some facet of the 'many-splendour'd thing' which is the truth of God. It is that element of teaching which rescues preaching from the danger of sensationalism, or emotionalism, or the merely histrionic.* Matthew, in describing Jesus' ministry in the local towns, indicates that that ministry combined the work of teaching and of preaching in a rich combination of assault on the darkness of the people (**Matthew 11.1**).

The word most commonly used when the evangelists speak of the preaching of Jesus was a lively one. It had within it the nuance of an announcement made by a herald, a proclamation with authority behind it, something which demanded a response. There is an urgency in Mark's description of Jesus coming into Galilee after his baptism and temptation. It was 'after John had been arrested.' (**Mark 1.14**) John's prophetic voice was silenced; his message had been too straight and uncomfortable, so the powers that be had to shut him up in prison. But the word of God must not be muzzled. Jesus would pick it up where John had been compelled to lay it down. 'After John had been arrested, Jesus came . . . proclaiming the gospel of God: "The time has arrived . . ." God's clock has struck. The great moment of history has arrived—'the year of the Lord's favour' of which Isaiah had spoken (**Isaiah 61.2**) and to which Jesus had referred in his first sermon (**Luke 4.19**). Things could never be the same again. A new day had dawned with the coming of the man from Nazareth.

He came as a herald, a man with his sovereign's authority behind him. Now a herald may be a bearer of bad news (the defeat of his king or the subjugation of his people by an enemy) or he may be the bearer of good news. There was no doubt about the nature of the news which this herald brought. It was *good* news. Jesus, so

---

*The Anglican bishop's 'throne' is misnamed. It is a *seat*, and a seat was the place where the teacher, in olden days, did his work. A bishop's seat is there to remind people that the bishop is a *teacher*—there to scatter the darkness of ignorance.

the Gospels insist again and again, brought good news—not a new list of burdens to be borne or of duties to be performed, but the announcement that God reigns! All that his hearers had to do was to turn round ('repent'), to stop running away from the king, to turn and face him in his loving majesty and believe in him with the trust of a child in its father. That message—so stunningly simple—had within it the power of dynamite. It had about it a note of urgency—there can be no apathy where the gospel is concerned.

The proclamation of Jesus was primarily about *God*—his care, his reign, his loving interference in our concerns. It is about the *living* God, not about a Sphinx-like deity who has not bothered to declare himself. It is about a God who has dared to expose his very nature, and let his mighty self be 'focused' for us; otherwise we should be dazzled beyond comprehension—in Jesus of Nazareth. In days gone by, God sent messengers who sought to carry his message to people. Now that means of communication has been transcended. God has spoken in his son. Jesus *is* what God has to say to people. He *is* God's final word. In him what is in God's mind, what is on God's heart, has been revealed. Look. Look long and hard. Here is revelation. Here is the 'good news'. Jesus is himself that news.

Teaching and preaching as he did, Jesus began to push back the tides of ignorance and sin.

Jesus the Healer—Let us watch him at his healing. Here again the three main activities of Jesus' ministry spill over one into another. *Teaching* can certainly be a healing activity. Many of us can look back to our young days and see how much suffering we should have been saved had we been rightly taught on this or that issue. More positively, we can look back and see what a liberation it was when some teacher came our way and pushed back a little of our ignorance and dispelled some part of our darkness. Our teacher was our healer. *Preaching*, too, can be a healing activity. Some of us are fortunate to be able to recall days when we sat spellbound under the preaching ministry of some man or woman of God. We said: 'If God is like *that*, if the gospel is like what I am hearing, then life—my life—takes on a wholly different hue. I am loved. I am liberated. I can be whole . . .'

So it was with the Servant-Son. As he taught and as he preached, healing came. 'God's in his heaven; all's right with the world'? No: nothing as facile as that. This teacher-preacher had no ready-made answer to life's great problems. But there was enough in his teaching and preaching to enable his hearers to look up, and breathe, and laugh, and live with a newness of life. Had he never laid his hands on anyone specifically to heal, there would have been healing in his words. 'The words I have spoken to you are both spirit and *life*.' (**John 6.63**, author's italics)

But there was more to the ministry of Jesus even than his teaching and preaching. Jesus had a strong sense of the power of touch. He put his arms round the children (**Mark 9.36; 10.16**); he touched the leper and the unclean (**Mark 1.41**); he put his fingers in the ears of the deaf (**Mark 7.33**); he took hold of the hand of Peter's feverish mother-in-law (**Mark 1.31**). Those hands, so gentle yet so firm, seemed to have the power to dissipate sickness and to convey wholeness, integration, health. He knew how to *handle* people. The forces of evil were rebuked—'This woman . . . who has been bound by Satan . . .', he said (**Luke 13.16**). The spoiler was despoiled. Those eyes could help to make people whole, as when he looked at Philip with rebuke—'Have I been all this time with you, Philip, and still you do not know me?' (**John 14.9**); or at Peter with loving disappointment when he denied him (**Luke 22.61**); or at the young quartet of Simon and Andrew, James and John by the lake with imperious invitation (**Mark 1.16–20**). His was a healing presence.

In these three main ways, then, the Servant-Son fought the threefold enemy of ignorance, sin, and disease: by his teaching, preaching and healing. He also took on to himself the burden of our sicknesses and sorrows. Jesus—Joshua—Saviour; Jesus—teacher, preacher, healer.

—— THE POSITIVE AIM ——

The *positive* aim of the healing ministry of Jesus was *to set in motion a process by which a man or woman could become a rounded personality,* open to development, a whole being, at *peace* with God, with other people, and with himself or herself.

Peace, a major word in the biblical writings, means much more than the ending of hostilities. We frequently use the word in that limited sense, as when we say at the end of some terrible international conflict: 'A peace treaty was signed.' That document probably left in its wake a legacy of hatred and resentment. The guns had stopped firing and the bombs had ceased to fall; but that was about all. The odds were that war might easily break out again. 'Peace' in the Bible and especially in the Gospels has a much more positive content to it than that. It can mean, in a communal sense, the total welfare of a nation. It can describe a community of persons who enjoy the smile of God and the delight of happy relationships one with another. There are no divisive rifts within that community. There is a wholeness about it which is creative and infectious. 'I alone know my purpose for you, says the Lord: *wellbeing* and not misfortune . . .' (**Jeremiah 29.11**, author's italics) Wellbeing: the word is *shalom*, peace. Such is God's attitude to his people.

At a more personal level, the word 'peace' is frequently used to indicate the cessation of a condition of brokenness, of inner conflict, of meaninglessness; and the entry into a new experience of integration and wholeness. It is the establishment of health.

Such was the ministry of Jesus. He was a minister of wholeness, health, holiness, *peace*. Let us look at five instances.

The Paralysed Man (**Mark 2.1–12**)

Mark sketches the scene graphically. It is early in the ministry of Jesus but word has got around that the young teacher also has healing gifts. The crowds gather round the place where he was living, blocking the way in. No matter; oriental roofs are made in such a way that the tiles can easily be taken up, and his friends can let the would-be patient down through the hole to the feet of Jesus—for the invalid is paralysed, and it takes four men to carry him on his floppy mattress. There he lies—the crowd has made way for him. He looks up—straight into the eyes of Jesus, compassionate eyes, loving eyes. Would he speak the word that the patient most longed to hear—'My son, your paralysis is cured: stand up, and walk'? No. For the skilled diagnosis of Jesus tells him that paralysis is not his primary problem: sin is. Deal with that, and the paralysis can be dealt with later. We need not delay to enquire what precisely was the sin which was holding up the forces of life:

that is beside the point. There it was; and Jesus proceeds to deal with it. 'My son, your sins are forgiven.' It was as if a load had been lifted, as if chains had been taken off him. He was free, released from what had inhibited him. Now he was ready for the enabling word: 'Stand up, take your bed, and walk.'

We must not be so foolish as to jump to false conclusions from this story: 'All suffering is the result of sin.' It is not as simple as that. There is much suffering for which the sufferers are *not* responsible—they were born with that disadvantage. The question that the disciples put to Jesus when they were confronted by the man blind from birth, 'Rabbi, who sinned, this man or his parents?' was met with the straight reply that none of them sinned (**John 9.1–5**). But that very frequently there is a connection—often a close connection—between sin and suffering is so obvious as to need little proving. If I abuse my body, which is a temple of the Holy Spirit, by smoking, or overeating, or overdrinking, I cannot blame God if I suffer. If I maintain an attitude of un-love towards a fellow human being, I should not be surprised if there is a physical or nervous reaction which is detrimental to my health. There are hundreds of beds in our hospitals which would be unoccupied if the patients in them got their relationships right with God or with other people. Wrong relationships are corrosive. Forgiveness is therapeutic. Get right with God: get right with your neighbour, and the benefit to your personal well-being may greatly surprise you. The straight words in the sermon on the mount: 'If you do not forgive others, then your Father will not forgive the wrongs that you have done' (**Matthew 6.15**) are not a threat, still less are they vengeful; they are simply a statement of fact. The universe is made that way: don't pit yourself against it. You will only get hurt if you do. 'It is hard *for you*, this kicking against the goad' (**Acts 26.14**, NEB, author's italics).

We have seen that, in the case of the paralysed man, there was clearly some sin which was blocking his healing. Jesus, with his clarity of diagnosis and his sure touch, deals with this first. He declares forgiveness. He releases the man. Physical strength seeps in. The paralysis is cured. The man stands up. He walks—and the crowd marvels and praises God.

The Crippled Woman (Luke 13.10–17)

The story of the woman 'crippled . . . for eighteen years . . . bent double and quite unable to stand up straight' introduces us to some features which are absent from the story of the paralytic which we have just been considering. There is no suggestion that the woman herself made an approach to Jesus, seeking his healing touch, nor that her friends brought her into his presence (as the paralytic's friends did). Jesus takes the initiative—'When Jesus saw her he called her' (Luke 13.12). This minister of health and wholeness is on the warpath. It is not right that 'this woman, a daughter of Abraham' should go on like this—unable to look up and see people eye to eye, prevented from seeing the sun and the trees . . . Satan, people's great enemy, has been at work; he has been binding her for eighteen long years. She must be loosed from his clutches.

The language is, of course, pictorial but it is very powerful. There are many who, faced with a situation such as this, would react in a very different way. They would say: 'This sickness is the will of God. She must accept and bear it, if it may be without complaint or bitterness.' Jesus takes the way of resistance, of opposition, of offensive action. The forces of life and light must be pitted against the forces of disease and darkness.

The story does not stand alone. Mark tells the tale of a leper who sought the healing help of Jesus—'If only you will, you can make me clean'. We must note Mark's comment—Jesus was *moved to anger*; he stretched out his hand, and said, 'I will; be clean.' (Mark 1.41) Why this anger? Because this poor wreck of a man was not what God intended him to be. God is on the side of health and is at work to further the healing process. Jesus is engaged in continuing that work. The man goes out *clean*, able to mix once again in society, whole!*

In John's story of the raising of Lazarus, there is a similar emphasis on the Servant-Son's distress in the presence of Lazarus' death—'He was moved with indignation and deeply distressed . . . Jesus wept . . .

---

*This comment on **Mark 1.41** will puzzle those whose versions of the story give some such translation as 'moved with compassion' instead of 'moved to anger'. Two different words are used in the Greek manuscripts. On the principle that, in such cases, the more difficult word is the more likely to be the right one, the *Revised English Bible* has decided on 'moved to anger'.

Jesus, again deeply moved, went to the tomb . . .' (**John 11.33, 35, 38**) No resignation here! The Lord of life takes action. He issues commands: 'Take away the stone.' (**John 11.39**) 'Lazarus, come out.' (**John 11.43**) 'Loose him; let him go.' (**John 11.44**)

The evangelists seek to give us the picture of Jesus as a warrior, in conflict with the power of sin and darkness and disease, in order to bring peace and wholeness to those who are their victims.

The Mad Man (**Luke 8.26–39**)

The two stories we have been looking at were stories of rescue from *physical* troubles—paralysis and spinal curvature. This story is about a man with severe mental derangement—unable to mix with society, at home only with the dead (**Luke 8.27**); distressed in the presence of Jesus even to the point of extreme fear; chained, 'for safety's sake', but endowed with demonic strength to break loose again and again.

Jesus manages to get him sufficiently quiet to put a question to him—'What is your name?' Contact has been made. Interest has been shown. Two men are in dialogue one with the other—the wreck of a man with the Lord of peace. 'What is your name?' To a Jew at that time his name meant much more than a name normally does to us; it was a pointer to his character, to what he was at heart. The one-word answer spoke volumes—'Legion', he said. A legion was a unit of the Roman army numbering several thousand men. In giving this reply, the maniac was saying in effect: 'I'm not just a man. I'm a multitude, a mob. And all the members of the mob are at war with one another. I'm a wreck.'

The story of the exit of the torturing demons from the man and their entry into the pigs is difficult for us modern westerners to appreciate. Nor does it matter very much for our present purpose. The climax of the story comes in **Luke 8.35**, where the locals came out to see what had been happening. 'They came to Jesus, and found the man from whom the demons had gone out sitting at his feet clothed and in his right mind . . .' No wonder that 'the man went all over the town proclaiming what Jesus had done for him.' (**Luke 8.39**)

'*Mens sana in corpore sano*—a sound mind in a sound body'. Juvenal's prayer expressed better than he knew God's ideal for his children. Jesus set about making it a reality, and in these cases of physical and mental healing gave us a foretaste of the coming kingdom when there will be no more mourning and crying and pain, for the old order will have passed away (**Revelation 21.4**).

The Immoral Woman (**Luke 7.36–50**)

We pass in this story from physical and mental to moral healing.

The story begins at a dinner party at which Jesus was a guest. We can easily picture the dinner, given perhaps on the patio of the big house, making it possible for an outsider to approach with no difficulty. The party was going well except for the intrusion of a woman who would insist on making an exhibition of herself and of her devotion to the guest of the evening! And what a woman—'A woman who was living an immoral life in the town' (**Luke 7.37**), 'a bad character' (**Luke 7.39**)! What a scene! It was most unseemly. Had the guest been a real prophet as some were saying he was, he would have known what sort of woman this was and would have put a stop to the demonstration. So they said. Jesus turned to his host. 'You see this woman?' Compare her lavish love with your chilly reception. 'Her great love proves that her many sins have been forgiven' (can you see the flush rising to the host's face?); 'where little has been forgiven, little love is shown'. This was high drama. But the best is kept to the last. Jesus turns from the host to the uninvited guest—the woman off the street—with a declaration and an invitation. The *declaration* is brief—'Your sins are forgiven'—but the outcome is miraculous. For how long had these sins burdened her, like a load hung round her neck; and the more she strove the deeper she got in the mire. Now she is free—*forgiven*! The *invitation* is all grace—'Your faith has saved you; *go in peace.*' 'Go *into* peace', so says the Greek text here. There is motion in that invitation: move out of the past into the future. You will discover a new and different world, a world where grace reigns, where strength is given, where God takes over.

The story leaves so much unsaid. What happened to the woman after her restoration? Did the Pharisee heed the rebuke given by his guest? Did he see the point of the little parable of the two debtors which Jesus slipped into the conversation with such penetrating skill? (**Luke 7.41–42**) Our curiosity must remain unsatisfied. We know that a woman, deeply in need, found her need met when she came into contact with the saving ministry of the healing Christ. She entered into wholeness, peace. That is what matters.

The Samaritan Woman (**John 4.1–42**)

With great skill and with considerable detail John tells the story of another encounter between Jesus and a woman in need. He makes us feel the heat of the occasion—'It was about noon, and Jesus, tired after his journey' (from Judaea to a Samaritan town on his way to Galilee) 'was sitting by the well'. Alone, of course; noon was no time for drawing water; that is done in the cool of early morning and of evening. Alone, except for one woman. John makes us share the surprise of the situation—Jesus engaging in conversation with a woman, and she a member of the hated Samaritan people! Why was she there alone? Presumably because she wanted to avoid the sneers of those who knew more than she could have wished about her past. Anyway, this Jewish young man, passing through her town, would know nothing of that—she was safe with *him*. Well, there he was, obviously hot and thirsty and in need of a drink. 'Give me a drink', he said. Half playfully, half seriously, she expresses her surprise— only to find that the stranger is ministering to *her* and talking of the deep things of life: human need, eternal life, and how he would give *her* a drink of water that would be everlastingly fresh. He rouses her sense of need—'Sir, give me this water . . .'

The healing Christ is at work with this needy woman. But some- times doctors, if they are truly to do their work, have to use the knife if their patient is to be fully healed. 'Go and call your husband . . .' It was like a surgeon's thrust: 'You are right in saying that you have no husband, for though you have had five husbands, the man you are living with now is not your husband.' (**John 4.18**) How did he know? Why was he touching this sore spot? Must he press so hard?

It was the touch of love: the love that will not evade the issue, the love that will not let us go but works away until the wound is healthy and God can do his restorative work. For her that moment came when she discovered who it was that was ministering to her, 'the Messiah' who was speaking to her (**John 4.26**). That is the saving discovery which makes a broken woman into a shining witness, back among her Samaritan friends. She 'left her water-jar'—a nice touch; she had business to do which brooked no delay. She went off to the town. 'Come and see a man . . . Could this be the Messiah?' Soon there was a crowd around the well, listening to the man who had brought health and wholeness to the woman.

Here is the story of a miracle—a woman, rejected by society, accepted by Christ, newborn by the Spirit's touch. She is no theologian; she has never been to a class on evangelism or to an evangelistic rally. But her eyes have been opened to see the wonder of the man she has met at the well, and her lips have been opened—not to give a lecture but with infinite tact to say to the people who had scorned her: 'Come and see . . . Could this be . . .?' John comments: 'Many Samaritans of that town came to believe in him because of the woman's testimony'—just that and nothing more. That opened the way for Jesus to speak the healing re-creative word—'Many more became believers because of what they heard *from his own lips*.' This led these people to say to the woman, frankly and without flattering: 'It is no longer because of what *you* said that we believe, for we have heard him ourselves; and we are convinced that he is the Saviour of the world.' (**John 4.42**, author's italics.)

—— *QUESTIONS* ——

1 Jesus, as he went about his work of teaching, preaching, and healing, did so with authority. This authority surprised people. How would you describe it? Of what did it consist?

2 What do you consider to be the essential ingredients of a sermon? Wherein does a sermon differ from, say, a college lecture or a secular address?

3 God is the source of all wisdom and knowledge. What bearing has this on our attitude to new knowledge? What has it to say about the church's part in the education of our people—adult and young?

4 God is the source of all health. What does this suggest as to the relationship between the state agencies for health and security and the outreach of the church, not only centrally but also in your neighbourhood?

5 What main lessons may we learn from a study of the five instances of Jesus' healing ministry outlined on pp. 66–72?

—— PRAYERS ——

We pray for those who teach and preach,
        that through our ministry, healing may come.
        May we be given clarity of mind
                        incisiveness of speech
                        lively imagination
                        perception of need.

    Take our minds, and think through them.
    Take our lips, and speak through them.
    Take our hearts, and set them on fire with love for thee.
    What we know not, teach us,
    What we have not, give us,
    What we are not, make us,
    For Jesus Christ's sake.

We pray for those engaged in the ministry of medicine:
    Heavenly Father,
        we know that all healing comes from you, and so we ask your
        blessing on all engaged in the ministry of healing.
    We pray for doctors, nurses, paramedics,
        for the staff who work in our hospitals,
        and for those who tend the sick in their homes.
    Give them the wisdom, skill, and patience that they need.
    May they know that in ministering to the sick they are fellow-workers
        with you and are furthering your purposes of love:
        through Jesus Christ our Lord.

Eternal God, whose Son Jesus Christ bore our griefs and carried our
        sorrows, and still comes to us in the guise of the needy, we pray for
        those in distress,
                the hungry and the homeless,
                the incapacitated and the handicapped,
                the mentally afflicted and the depressed,
                the weary and the dying,
                the lonely and the bereaved.

Help us who offer these prayers to take the suffering of others on ourselves, and so, by your grace, to become the agents of your transforming love; through Jesus Christ our Lord.

God our Father,
    You are the source of all health and healing,
                all strength and peace.
    Teach us to know you more clearly
        and to trust you more firmly.
    Take from us all that hinders your healing power,
        all anxieties and fears.
    Help us in our weakness to rest in your love
        and to enter into the stillness of your presence;
    through Jesus Christ our Lord.

Lord, still me.
Let my mind be enquiring, searching.
Let my heart be open.
Save me from mental rust.
Deliver me from spiritual decay.
Keep me alive and alert.
Teach me, that I may reach others.

May God himself, the God of peace,
    make you holy through and through,
    keep you sound in spirit, soul and body,
    free of any fault when our Lord Jesus Christ comes.
    He who calls you keeps faith; he will do it.[1]

—— *NOTE* ——

This has been a long chapter, but I hope a fruitful one.

It might be well to pause at this point:

to look at the summary at the beginning of the chapter; (p. 58)
to glance over the chapter again;
to note any things which have struck you as new or as specially valuable.

Take time for a breather.

Then you will be ready for the next lap, 'Dramatist'. I think you will enjoy it.

Dramatist

In this chapter, we note that Jesus got his message across to people not only by the use of words but also by dramatic action.

His coming to us all as a human being was itself 'the greatest drama ever staged', and reached its climax in the cross and resurrection.

We select for study three of his dramatic actions:

The cleansing of the temple (**Mark 11.15–18**. See also **John 2.13–22**. pp. 80–82)

The entry into Jerusalem (**Mark 11.1–11**. pp. 82–84)

The foot-washing (**John 13.1–17**. pp. 84–86)

We watch some modern instances of Christian drama (pp. 87–89).

Drama means literally 'what is *done*, acted out, performed'. To say the word 'drama' is to see a stage, with actors engaged in doing something which it would be impossible to convey by words alone. Words go far—but only so far. Drama is an acknowledgment of the indequacy of words to convey what is in the mind or on the heart of the writer or author.*

Life is full of drama. Laughter is drama, a physical expression—be it a guffaw or a chuckle—of an inner amusement which has to 'come out'. Sympathy can be expressed in words; but how often it can*not*! When we feel most deeply, words most often fail us. We resort to a pressing of the hand, a hug, a kiss—and that *does* more than any speech however deeply felt or carefully prepared. Sexual intercourse is the acting out of a love too deep for words between a man and a woman who have covenanted with one another till death parts them. That most sacred act says what words cannot.

The Bible is full of drama. Some of the greatest dramatists were the prophets who were content to make fools of themselves if, by their dramatic actions, they could convey divine truth. We think, for example, of Jeremiah with 'the cords and crossbars of a yoke' on his neck, to symbolize the bondage of nations under the yoke of Babylon's king **(Jeremiah 27–28)**; or again of Jeremiah buying from the potter an earthenware jar and smashing it before the eyes of the men who accompanied him, to say more vividly than words could do, that God was about to smash the princes of Judah and citizens of Jerusalem who had engaged in the worship of Baal **(Jeremiah 19)**.

'The greatest drama ever staged', as Dorothy Sayers put it, was the incarnation of the son of God. Perhaps the greatest passage ever written is to be found in the opening eighteen verses of John's Gospel—all the more stunning for the simplicity of the language used to portray it. 'The Word . . . what God was'—the life that was 'the light of mankind', the light which 'shines in the darkness', itself never being mastered—that 'Word became flesh'. That Word became the stuff of which we humans are made, not despising our humanity though we had spoiled its purity, but ennobling it, sancti-

---

*Similarly, *opera* is a Latin word which means *works*—an admission, if you will, that words alone have failed: now is the time for deeds, works, visible activity.

fying it, and making it the medium through which the mind and heart of God could be bared for us to see and to know. What no words could say, the Word made flesh *did*. That is drama at its highest.

And at its lowest. 'The eternal Word not able to speak a word', as Bishop Lancelot Andrewes put it. That Word 'made his home among us', so says the *Revised English Bible*; and that is a good translation so far as it goes. But what sort of 'home' was it? It might have been a palace or a luxury villa. The Greek text has no doubt about the answer to that question. Jesus 'pitched his tent' among us. Was the writer thinking of the tent of meeting made so much of in the Old Testament (see, for example, **Exodus 33.7–11**), where God met his people in their wilderness journeyings? Maybe: for Bethlehem is the meeting place where God in his mercy disclosed himself to humans in their need. But 'pitched his tent' means something more down-to-earth than this. A tent, as any camper will tell you, is a frail thing, liable to be penetrated by the rain or, at its worst, to be blown away. A tent in its very nature speaks of fragility, of vulnerability. Such was the 'flesh' which the Servant-Son took on. 'Bearing the human likeness, sharing the human lot, he humbled himself'—Paul, in these words (**Philippians 2.7–8**), might be commenting on John's 'pitched his tent'.

'He pitched his tent among us, and we saw his . . .' *humiliation*, surely? Not so. 'His *glory*' (**John 1.14**, author's italics). No human eye dare look on the naked glory of God. But if his very being is disclosed in the babe at Bethlehem, we dare to look and see, in the frailty and vulnerability of the Word made flesh, the glory of God. This is a major theme in this fourth Gospel; it is announced in this verse, though we cannot develop it here, 'Anyone who has seen me has seen the Father' (**John 14.9**).

The verse about Jesus' glory (**John 1.14**) is not the climax of the prologue of the Gospel. That is reserved for **John 1.18**—'No one has ever seen God; God's only Son . . . has *made him known*'—another lovely word: 'has *exegeted* him'. Exegesis is the task of a language teacher who, faced with a class of students poring over a text in a foreign language, seeks to unpack the meaning of that text, to expose its secrets and make them available to the understanding of the students. The teacher is rewarded when he sees a light in the eyes of one of his students—'I'd never seen it like that before. Now I've got it! You have spelt it out for me.'

We have seen, in Chapter 6, how Jesus got to work as a minister of wholeness, using the media of teaching, preaching, and healing. Mighty media they were. But what he *was* conveyed more than what he did. It was the presence of the Word who was life and light that scattered the darkness; the powers of evil could not stand in his presence. In him the reign of God was displayed among the sons and daughters of men. 'It is I', he said, and the stormy waters ceased to rage (**Matthew 14.22–27**). In a real sense he *was* God's drama—the enactment on the stage of history of what God had to say to humans, the exposure of his heart and mind.

I want to take this idea of drama a stage further. Jesus was himself a dramatist. He knew the power of words, and no one ever used them with greater force than he did. But he knew also the limitation of words; he felt their inadequacy to convey what was longing to get out from within him; he knew the failure of words by themselves to say what needed to be said. How was he to *show* other people the essential meaning of his mission which to *him* had been made so clear at his baptism and at his temptation? The answer to that question was this: Jesus would *act*, perform, do things in a way which would not need many words of explanation. The deeds would say what a multitude of words would not. Jesus would be a *drama*tist. He would be the act-or. I take three examples:

——— THE CLEANSING OF THE TEMPLE* ———

We think of Jesus as exercising the major part of his ministry in the north of the Holy Land—in Galilee. That no doubt was the case. But there are pretty clear indications that he spent a considerable amount of time in the temple courts at Jerusalem, especially when

---

*We need not delay to enquire why John places this incident at the beginning of the ministry of Jesus while the other evangelists put it near the end (**John 2.13–22; Mark 11.15–18**). That would be an interesting exercise, but it does not affect our present purpose.

the city was full of travellers who had come up for the feasts. Many of those who frequented those courts would be better educated, more sophisticated, than the country people in the north, and the heart of Jesus went out to all alike. No doubt he prayed that the people from abroad who listened to him might respond and be the means by which God's 'salvation may reach earth's farthest bounds', as the servant song had said (**Isaiah 49.6**). Anyway, he cared for Jerusalem and for the great temple at its heart. 'O Jerusalem, Jerusalem . . . *how often* have I longed to gather your children . . . but you would not let me.' (**Luke 13.34**, author's italics) Luke records that 'his days were given to teaching in the temple . . . and the people flocked to listen to him in the temple.' (**Luke 21.37, 38**) Matthew records Jesus speaking to the crowd: 'Day after day I sat teaching in the temple . . .' (**Matthew 26.55**)

The deeper one's love for a person or an institution, the deeper is one's grief at their failure. As Jesus watched the ceaseless round of sacrifices, the offering of beasts and birds and cereals, he must have questioned the reality of the worship offered by many people and asked how many who had made their contributions went away at peace with God and in harmony with their neighbours, whole with the wholeness of God? Was *this* real religion? We get indications of two reactions on the part of Jesus to the temple and what went on in it:

First, there was *blazing indignation*. This was sparked off by the trading which went on in its courts (**Mark 11.15–18**, see also **Matthew 21.12–13** and **John 2.13–22**). It was high drama when Jesus drove the money-changers out and it involved huge courage to do so—'My house . . . a house of prayer . . . made a robbers' cave'! The commercializing of religion is not a pretty sight—in the eyes of God. The temple had been defiled. It must be cleansed. It is significant that Matthew, immediately after telling the story of the cleansing, says: 'In the temple the blind and the crippled came to him (Jesus), and he healed them.' *That* was what the temple was for—healing, not trading; salvation, not shekels; men and women in the totality of their personalities, not marketing.

Second, there were *tears*. If righteous anger is the reverse side of holy love, tears are the outward expression of that love. Jesus shed tears of grief over that city whose central glory was its temple: 'O Jerusalem, Jerusalem . . . how often have I longed to gather your children, as a hen gathers her brood under her wings; but you would not let me.' (Luke 13.34) The words are so familiar that their pathos is sometimes lost on us. The words that follow them are terrifying: 'Look! There is your temple, forsaken by God . . .' *Your* temple? No longer God's? A God-forsaken temple . . .? Matthew records that, after the cleansing of the temple, and the hostile reaction of the religious authorities to Jesus' healing work, 'he left them and went out of the city to Bethany, where he spent the night.' (Matthew 21.17) No comment—'He left them', temple, priests, scribes, the cold heartless religion—and 'went to Bethany': Mary, Martha, and Lazarus would understand . . . There would be warmth in the Bethany home.

Jesus the dramatist was at work in that cleansing act—the eyes flashing in anger and the eyes overflowing with tears *said* things to the observer which no words could convey.

———— THE ENTRY INTO JERUSALEM ————

Tucked away in John's Gospel is a verse which is relevant to our present subject: 'Jesus, realizing that they (the crowds) meant to come and seize him to proclaim him king, withdrew again to the hills by himself.' (John 6.15) It follows the story of the feeding of the five thousand. The popularity of Jesus was high. The people's physical needs had been met, and they were grateful: 'This is the kind of leader we want. Mount him on a charger. Make him a king. Maybe, with a bit of luck, he might drive the hated Romans into the sea. Home rule for Israel!'

Jesus would have none of it. He had wrestled with precisely that issue in his temptation in the desert. He had decided *against* the way of power and *for* the way of service. When the devil had shown him 'all the kingdoms of the world in their glory', his reply had been a peremptory 'Out of my sight, Satan!' (Matthew 4.8–10) Now the temptation was at him again. Recognizing it for what it was, subtle in its appeal, recurring in its intensity, he 'withdrew again to the hills—by himself', there to meet with his God and to renew his covenant relationship with him as his Servant-Son.

This concept of Servant-Son dominated the years of Jesus' public ministry. If he himself found it difficult to be obedient to it, he found it even more difficult to explain and expound to his followers. He taught it by word constantly, but that was not enough. He must dramatize it.

Mark 9.30–37 sketches for us a little scene which is half humorous, half pathetic. The master and the disciples were on the road; perhaps Jesus was striding ahead. A few steps behind him, but not near enough for him to hear their words, the disciples were engaged in a heated argument. They all reached Capernaum and went indoors. 'What were you arguing about on the way?' They looked sheepish and ashamed—'They had been discussing which of them was the greatest.' We can hear it—Peter makes an obvious claim: '*I* am the greatest', like an ancient Mohammed Ali! 'No, he's not, *I* am', says another. How can the master show the folly of it all? He *dramatizes* it, calls a little child and sets him in front of them as a living object-lesson, puts his arm round the child and says to them: 'Look . . .'

Albert Nolan* makes the point that, contrary to popular opinion, the image of the little child is not an image of innocence. Rather, the child is a live parable of 'littleness', *the opposite of status and prestige*. In the society of Jesus' day, children had no status at all—they did not count. But for Jesus they *did* count—they were real people—to such as these 'the kingdom of God belongs' (**Mark 10.14**). The broken people, the poor, the oppressed, the prostitutes, the tax collectors, those without status, *and* those who were prepared to abandon claims to greatness or to make claims for first places in society, the kingdom belongs to *them*. The status-less child, with Jesus' arm around him, said more to that arguing group than any words could say. Status and prestige are not in the vocabulary of the followers of Jesus.

The dramatizing of this truth reaches its climax in the story of the entry of Jesus into Jerusalem (**Mark 11.1–11; Matthew 21.1–9; Luke 19.28–38; John 12.12–19**). The ministry of Jesus is moving towards its climax, his 'hour' (as John puts it) is near. Now is the moment for an action that will speak to all the crowds. Pilgrims to the festivals in Jerusalem were expected to enter the city *on foot*. Jesus will *ride* in. No wonder the crowds gather round and start not

---

*Albert Nolan, *Jesus before Christianity*, (Orbis Books, Maryknoll, New York, 1976) pp. 54ff.

only to acclaim him but to carpet the road with their cloaks and to cut branches from the trees to spread in his path. The prophet Zechariah, in a passage which was interpreted as referring to a coming Messiah, had spoken of 'your king . . . coming to you, his cause won, his victory gained, humble and mounted on a donkey, on a colt, the foal of a donkey' (Zechariah 9.9). That picture must have puzzled those in the crowd who were well-enough versed in their Scriptures to recognize the saying in the prophecy. 'A king on a donkey'? Anyhow, better than nothing! There was something regal about him that day; and look at what he had achieved, and how he had taught, and how he had healed . . . It would be easy enough to exchange that lowly little beast for a charger. 'Hosanna'—the word, originally an exclamatory prayer meaning 'save now', had come to mean little more than 'hoorah!' Emotion ran high. 'What hope rebellion? Home rule for Israel!'

The lowly donkey held no embarrassment for its rider. He had deliberately chosen it and sent for it. There was that in the prophecy of Zechariah which said just what Jesus wanted to say. *No* charger for the Servant-Son! *No* regal panoply! A donkey was a servant-beast, a beast of burden, there to carry away the waste of society, the debris, the dirty, the smelly.

Jesus was not deceived by the acclamation of the crowds. He knew how fickle they could be. Today's 'hosanna' could be tomorrow's 'crucify'. Leave it at that—let the picture of the Messiah on a donkey register on their minds: they might recall it later and the picture of the Servant-Son would take on its true significance.

THE FOOT-WASHING

John has no story of the institution of the Eucharist. At the point in his Gospel where we might have expected to find that story, we are given the narrative of the washing of the disciples' feet by Jesus. John 13 is a remarkable chapter. It includes a grievous passage about Judas' forthcoming betrayal of his master, and about Simon Peter's protestation of lifelong faithfulness. All this is prefaced by the story of the foot-washing which occupies John 13.1–17.

'It was before the Passover festival.' With a sure touch, John sounds the note of sacrifice: Passover time when the lambs were slain. The greatest sacrifice is imminent.

'Jesus knew that his hour had come.' He had had to remind his mother, at the start of his ministry, that that 'hour had not yet come' (John 2.4). Later on, he could not be seized by opponents 'because his appointed hour had not yet come' (John 7.30; 8.20). But as he approaches Jerusalem, the clouds darken; he is conscious that the hour is drawing nearer; now it 'has come' (John 12.23; 13.1). The 'hour' means the consummation of all his ministry on the cross—so the opening verse of John 13 is the evangelist's way of introducing the passion story—'He must leave this world and go to the Father'—for passion, resurrection, and ascension are one inseparable event.

'He had always loved his own who were in the world'—the whole story of his life and ministry bore witness to that—'and he loved them to the end.' Not simply to the end of his ministry. The word 'end' has more than a *temporal* significance here. 'To the uttermost' would not be an exaggeration—the uttermost to which the Servant-Son could go in service, namely, the washing of the disciples' feet, and that as a prelude to his sacrifice on the cross. The verb 'he loved them' has about it a hint of once-ness—'he demonstrated his love', the love to the uttermost. How? In the foot-washing. The *Jerusalem Bible* (1966), anxious to make these points clear to its readers, ventured a paraphrase: 'and now he showed how perfect his love was'.

The devil had already put it into the mind of Judas son of Simon Iscariot to betray him (John 13.2). The backcloth to the drama needs nothing to be added to this; great is the mystery of iniquity. Now we move straight from the demonic to the majestic: 'Jesus, well aware that the Father had entrusted everything to him, and that he had come from God and was going back to God'—here is sonship at its loftiest. This man, who has gathered his friends round him for a final meal, is the apostolic delegate of the father-God, entrusted with his mission to the world. This man is conscious that his task is set between the eternities—he came from God; he was going back to God. This man 'rose from the supper table' and—? Donned his regal garments? Surely. Seated himself on a throne? No. 'Took off his outer garment and, taking a towel, tied it round him. Then he poured water into a basin, and began to wash his disciples' feet and to wipe them with the towel.'

As I write, I try to picture the scene. I think it is a scene of complete silence. An exchange of glances between the disciples, perhaps. Raised eyebrows, certainly. Who had ever seen or imagined such a drama? The teacher and Lord doing the menial task which in any society would be left to the lowest servant? But this is a total reversal of values, an abandonment of status, a revolution. It is left to Simon Peter to break the silence—he had a way of doing that! Even *his* voice is husky; he is shaken to his roots: 'You, Lord, washing *my* feet?'

The status-less child round whom he had put his arm; the silly, smelly donkey on which he had ridden into the city; had the disciples missed the point of these dramatic acts? Surely they could not fail to see the meaning of this, the greatest drama of all. 'If I, your Lord and Teacher, have washed your feet, you also ought to wash one another's feet.' (John 13.14) He had *told* them this again and again:

> You know that among the Gentiles the recognized rulers lord it over their subjects, and the great make their authority felt. It shall not be so with you; among you, whoever wants to be great must be your servant, and whoever wants to be first must be the slave of all. (Mark 10.42–44)

Yes, they had heard it all. Yes, they had nodded their heads in assent. But it had hardly registered—not even when Jesus had added: 'The Son of Man did not come to be served but to serve, and to give his life as a ransom for many.' (Mark 10.45) But *now*—it was different: he was acting out the serving. He was dramatizing the teaching, he himself, Lord and teacher.

The greatest drama was yet to be staged—and until they had watched it enacted in blood and horror on the cross, it did not dawn in all its power. 'If I . . . you also . . .'

Paul was to speak of the crucifixion of Jesus as an open display—a drama indeed! 'Jesus Christ was openly displayed on the cross.'(Galatians 3.1) That crucified body was a public proclamation for all to read—an enactment in human weakness of the power of God's love. By the time Jesus reached the cross, he had ceased doing things; he had reached the point where he could only have things done *to* him. But was the infinite power of love ever seen more clearly than in that offering on the cross? There the negative 'cosmic powers' of sin and hatred were 'disarmed' (**Colossians 2.15**).

—— CHRISTIAN DRAMA TODAY ——

Anyone who is daring enough to attempt to write about the enormous themes on which we are engaged in this book is conscious of the inadequacy of words. He is using a medium whose limitations are obvious. That indeed is the subject of this book—that God's heart of love could not be exposed in words, it had to be enacted in human flesh, it had to be dramatized in the person of the Servant-Son.

What I would like to do would be to stop writing; to slip my arm through yours, the reader's; to take you with me (actually in two instances it would involve a flight across the Atlantic); to show you certain things, and then to say: 'I've finished using words. Look! Look deeply, until you see the meaning of what I am showing you— and then take what action you think is right.' As I cannot take you with me, I will describe, as briefly as I can, three scenes:

—— *Scene 1* ——

The location is Washington DC, USA. The backdrop is the cathedral, a building begun in the early years of this century, completed only a few years ago. Massive, it towers over the city. Like Solomon's temple, it is 'exceeding magnifical', a monument to human creative powers in stone and glass and manifold craft. It *could* be—God forbid!—a bit triumphalist: see what people can do! But there it stands—to the greater glory of God, we trust. Majestic, powerful.

Descend the steps outside the cathedral, cross the narrow road, and the visitor may enter a lovely garden. Tucked away, almost hidden amongst the shrubs and flowers, is a sculpture. It takes the viewer a little while to discern its meaning. There are two men held together, I had almost said intertwined, in a mighty embrace. The one is old, the other young, dishevelled. It is the home-coming of the prodigal son. I suppose the cathedral authorities could have installed a system, such as is used in many art galleries, by which, through headphones, a voice would tell you what the sculpture is all about, who carved it, what it cost. But that would be wholly out of place. Nor is it needed. The silent sculpture invites you to look. Look again. And again. What do you make of *that*? Unconditional love at work. No rebukes. No questions. A mighty welcome home. 'This son of mine was dead and has come back to life; he was lost and is found.' Let the festivities begin! 'There is joy among the angels of God over one sinner who repents . . .' (**Luke 15.10–32**)

We call it the parable of the prodigal son. It would be better to call it the parable of the prodigal father—prodigal with his love, lavish with his tenderness.

Well, there it stands, that sculpture, semi-hidden, down in a kind of lowly dell in the garden. It has nothing of the magnificence of the cathedral that towers above it. But would it be heretical to suggest that to some heavy-laden soul it *says* more, in its silence, about the God who so loves the world that he gave his son, than the towering church across the road? A drama in stone . . .

———— *Scene 2* ————

The location is, again, America. A lovely home, set in an idyllic surround of forest, of nature at her loveliest. The house was large and beautifully furnished. It housed a retired bishop and his wife, gracious in their hospitality. There one could enjoy music, art, laughter, prayer—all the good things that make life rich. 'Before you go over to the church', the bishop said to me on the Sunday morning, 'I'd like to take you downstairs.' We went together. The room had been a jacuzzi—for English readers I refer them to the dictionary: 'a bath or pool' equipped with 'underwater jets that keep the water . . . constantly agitated'. Now it was the bishop's chapel—a simple room, equipped with moveable chairs. It was the central feature which gripped my attention.

In the middle of the room was the table, where the eucharist was celebrated, a dramatic setting forth of the gospel through the elements of the bread and the wine. But—and this I had never seen anywhere before—underneath that table, on the floor of the chapel, stood a basin and a jug and a towel. That was all. But it was everything. It spoke to me that morning as no spoken word could have done. 'So *that* is what it is all about. *That* is what the Servant-Son did immediately before he went out to his death—'He took off his outer garment and, taking a towel, tied it round him. Then he poured water into a basin . . .' And *that* is what the church is all about—'I have set you an example: you are to do as I have done for you.'

The bishop and I went over to the church that morning deep in thought.

—— *Scene 3* ——

I must admit that I have never been present at the scene which I am about to describe, though I am assured that it is a reality in countries overseas such as India and is enacted occasionally in England.

It is Sunday morning and the setting is that of a cathedral. The church is full. People have gathered, some from quite a distance, to share in a service of ordination. There in the front pews are the candidates, called, chosen, trained, and now ready to receive the laying on of hands for the office and work of a deacon or priest in the church of God. The service is awe-inspiring, and underneath the cassocks of many of the candidates there are shaking knees. But they know that the God who has called them is faithful, and their friends are supporting them with their prayers. The glorious music is in itself a strength. Here in this place God has met with his people over long centuries. They are surrounded with a great cloud of witnesses.

The central figure of the service is the bishop, the father-in-God of his people. He prays: 'Hear our prayer for your faithful people that each in his vocation and ministry may be an instrument of your love . . .' 'Send down the Holy Spirit upon your servant . . .' 'Give them vision and discipline . . .'

The ordination is over. The Eucharist follows. The blessing ends the service. The sanctuary empties. But all is not over—today. The bishop is coming back. He has divested himself of his robes and is dressed in a simple cassock. What is he about to do? He will begin to wash the disciples' feet and to wipe them with the towel. What was it the master said?: 'I have set you an example: you are to do as I have done for you.' 'If anyone wants to be first, he must make himself last of all and servant of all.' The bishop has acted this out in a drama for all to see. The silent drama has said it all.

——— QUESTIONS ———

1 Jesus used story (imagination) as a way to the heart and conscience. In your reckoning, which of his parables illustrates this approach most vividly?

2 God, who is love, seeks to penetrate our defences and get through to us—

        through ear-gate and eye-gate;
        through sacrament, worship, prayer;
        through music and silence;
        through drama and poetry;
        through reason;
        through friendship . . .

What means are proving most effective between God and you?

3 'Every time you eat this bread and drink the cup, you *proclaim* the death of the Lord, until he comes.' (**1 Corinthians 11.26**, author's italics) In what sense is the Eucharist (the Holy Communion, the Lord's supper, the Mass) a proclamation in the place where you worship? What would a visitor make of it? (see **1 Corinthians 14.25**)

4 Look again at the three scenes sketched on pp. 87–89. Look carefully. Drama is performed in order to elicit response. What response do the sketches elicit from you?—

        resentment?
        repentance?
        worship?
        resolve?
        what?

———— *PRAYERS* ————

Almighty God, who hast proclaimed thine eternal truth by the voice of prophets and evangelists: Direct and bless those who in this generation speak where many listen and write what many read; that they may do their part in making the heart of the people wise

its mind sound,
and its will righteous;
to the honour of Jesus Christ our Lord.[1]

Lord God, you have placed in human hearts great power for good or evil
through television.
We pray for those whose faces and voices are thus known in millions
of homes;
for those who decide policies and plan schedules;
and those who direct and produce programmes.
We pray that their skills and gifts may be devoted to what is true and good, so that those who watch and listen may be informed and enter-tained without being debased or corrupted; through Jesus Christ our Lord.[2]

I CLAIM YOUR POWER TO CREATE

O Ingenious One,
it is not only creation,
but creativity
that awes me.
It is a wondrous,
fearsome thing
that you share your power to create.

O Mysterious One,
I shrink from your power,
yet I claim it;
and it is mine by your genius
or madness,
this power to speak

and have light burst upon a mind
    or darkness descend upon a heart;
this power to make music
    to which souls dance
      or armies march;
this power to mold and paint and carve
    and so spin out the stars
      by which I plot my course to heaven or to hell;
this power to hear and touch and taste
    the love and truth
      by which life itself is birthed and built
        or the hate and lies
          by which it shrivels and dies.

O Daring One,
it is an awesome power you've shared;
and I rejoice in the artists
    who dare to use their gift
      to create the beauty which casts this world
        into a more whole and holy dimension,
    who dare to breathe visions and vibrations
      into dullness,
        as you breathed life into dust.

O Gracious One,
it is an awesome power you've shared;
and I honor your power
    not only in pianist, poet and painter,
      but in those whose encouragement ignites my heart,
        whose laughter lights up a room,
          whose touch fills a void,
            whose integrity inspires my will,
    whose commitment builds a church,
      whose compassion builds a community,
      whose demands stretch my soul,
        and whose love makes my day;
and I honor your power in those artists
    of kitchen and office and shop,

of courtroom and classroom and sickroom;
in those crazy people
who somehow know the world is always unfinished,
and who happily risk pushing and shoving
and tugging and pounding
and making love to it
until it and all of us
come out in more glorious shape.

O Ingenious One,
it is not only creation,
but creativity
that awes me.
It is a wondrous,
fearsome thing
that you share your power to create.[3]

Servant-Son Church

In this chapter, we see the early Christians at work, seeking to follow the Servant-Son and to further his life and work in their world.

We note the fourfold basis of their spiritual life in **Acts 2.41–47** (pp. 97–99).

The servant-sons/daughters of God have been given gifts by the Spirit.

We study **1 Corinthians 12.4–11**
2 Corinthians 4.5–6
Romans 8.14–17
1 John 3.1–3

The impression made by the life, death, and resurrection of the Servant-Son had been profound. The period of Jesus' public ministry had been short, for Jesus was only about thirty-three when he was crucified. But after his physical withdrawal (his 'ascension'), there remained a host of people who had met him and come under his influence. The extent of that influence varied greatly. On some it had been deep—Mary and the apostolic band being the most obvious examples. Jesus had not gone to all that trouble in training the twelve without leaving a group of men deeply marked in character, in their sense of priorities, in their attitudes to life. There were many *women*, in addition to Mary of Magdala, Joanna and Susanna whom Luke mentions (**Luke 8.2–3**), who had provided for Jesus out of their own resources and who, in doing so, had been touched to the depths of their beings (see also **Mark 15.40–41**).

There were those to whom Jesus appeared after his resurrection— 'Over five hundred of our brothers, most of whom' were 'still alive, though some have died', as Paul mentioned in a letter written in the early fifties AD (**1 Corinthians 15.6**). How many thousands, many of them young people, had hung on his words and watched him at his work, as he laboured in towns and villages and in the crowded temple courts in Jerusalem! They could not forget. Many of them had been revolutionized in their outlook on religion and on life by the personal impact and by the teaching of Jesus.

Then there was Pentecost when, in an astonishing way, the Spirit did his great work of taking the things of Jesus and making them known to people (see **John 16.14**). The first impressions were *fastened* in mind and conscience by that Spirit who was—and is—the other self of Jesus. Jesus to them was not just a memory; he was a living presence. The church, the members of the body of Christ, went to society as representatives of Jesus, to perpetuate the picture which he had painted, to commend the gospel he had proclaimed, to illustrate it in their own flesh and blood. They were engaged on an errand of love.

'As I have loved you, *so* you are to love one another.' (**John 13.34**, author's italics) Jesus had shown that love in a life and death of Servant-Sonship. Some of those who had seen him, heard him, and watched him at work had grasped that 'as . . . so' of the Servant-

Son. Others had failed to see what he was on about—how could suffering love be *the* criterion of Christian discipleship? Surely power tactics were right?

So the church went to the world. It was not a perfect church. There never has been such a thing. There never will be on this earth, for the church is for sinners, sinners on the road. It is always in the process of being reformed. Some people think of the early church as a model whose every mark is to be imitated, an almost perfect church which we must copy. The evidence will not support such a theory. There are signs in plenty, in the book of Acts and in the Epistles, of a church which was fallible and whose members were weak. A few examples will suffice.

What are we to make of the story of Ananias and Sapphira in **Acts 5**? Clearly this couple had sinned grievously in seeking to deceive their fellow disciples. But was Peter right in dealing with them in such terms that in no time they were both dead? Was not this the use of power-tactics which induced heart attacks, rather than love-tactics which sought to win the sinner back?

Again, there was a dispute about who should take whom on a missionary journey. The dispute was so sharp that Luke used a word which we know as 'paroxysm' to describe it (**Acts 15.39**). Barnabas and Paul were no doubt sincere in their motives, but scarcely Christian in their method of selection! Again Paul, that giant of a man, could lose his temper and call the high priest a 'whitewashed wall'. True, he apologized, and said he did not know the identity of the man whom he had insulted, but . . .! (**Acts 23.1–5**)

One has only to read Paul's two letters to the Corinthians to see a church afflicted with just the kind of sins which afflict the church of Christ today—division, immaturity, sexual immorality, disputes, insensitivity to others' weaknesses, and so on.

Yes: it was a sinning church which went to the world. But it was a church whose main ideals were clear in the minds of many of its members, and luminously clear in the writings of some of its leaders. The image of the Servant-Son remained. As Jesus had been, so his church, his body, should be. It was to be a church whose members were marked, above all else, as servant-sons and servant-daughters.

—— SPIRITUAL LIFE RESOURCES ——

If the world was to see the members of the church as *servants* of God and as its servants for Jesus' sake; if it was to see them as *sons and daughters* of God; it was essential that the basics of their spiritual life should be sound. There cannot be a healthy plant if the soil is poor or sour. The early church may have got some things wrong, but on this matter they were undoubtedly right. The basics of their spiritual life are outlined in **Acts 2.42**: 'They met constantly to hear the apostles teach and to share the common life, to break bread, and to pray.' This was the basis, sure, firm, fourfold, on which the life and witness of the church was founded.

—— Apostolic Teaching ——

The members of the early church knew that theirs was an historic faith. It was not based on sentiment or mere goodwill. Certain things had happened, at Bethlehem, at Nazareth, outside Jerusalem's wall; a life had been lived unique of its kind; a death-and-resurrection had taken place without parallel in history; a wind had blown in that upper room whose effects were felt daily and by increasing numbers of people. Only a few years later, a newcomer to the apostolic band, Paul, was to summarize the heart of the apostolic teaching in what sounds like a primitive creed—'That Christ died for our sins . . . that he was buried; that he was raised to life . . . that he appeared . . .' (**1 Corinthians 15.3–7**) Doctrine mattered. The early Christians could not sit loose to it, nor be unfaithful in its proclamation. They 'met constantly to hear' the teaching, to ponder on its magnificence, to assimilate its meaning, and to share its message.

—— The Common Life—the Fellowship ——

When Jesus set out on his public ministry, he did not choose one man whom he would train up as his successor. He chose a dozen, a *body* of men. But what a dozen! The risk was enormous, for the group had within it all the seeds of possible dis-integration—a civil servant (Matthew), four tradesmen (Simon and Andrew, James and John), a political activist (Simon the Zealot), a traitor (Judas), and so on.

But, different as they were one from the other and frequent as, no doubt, were their quarrels, Jesus knitted them into a fellowship. As in a bicycle wheel the spokes draw nearer to one another as they draw nearer to the hub, so the members of the apostolic band came to realise that their loyalty to their master drew them closer to one another. Not without many growing pains but surely and steadily a *fellowship* was being created strong enough, at Pentecost, to embrace a huge addition to their number and, later, the addition of that stormy petrel, Saul of Tarsus. A 'common life' was established, strong enough to withstand and even to profit by the tensions of its members. It issued in an attempt to 'hold everything in common', the sharers selling 'their property and possessions and distributing to everyone according to his need'. Was this the 'first, fine, careless rapture' of a rash discipleship? Maybe. But there is something splendid in its abandonment of privilege and in the joy of 'fellowship' gained at cost.

——— *Breaking Bread* ———

The phrase occurs again a few verses later (**Acts 2.46**), where, clearly, the reference is to homely meals where 'unaffected joy' abounded. We can picture these little gatherings of Christians sharing one another's hospitality when the presence of Christ was so real that, though unseen, he was the host and they the guests. Such meals were repetitions of the Emmaus experience (**Luke 24.28–32**).

But the phrase 'to break bread', in the context of **Acts 2.42**, has about it a strong eucharistic flavour. As 'they met constantly . . . to break bread', they were obeying their Lord's command to 'do this in remembrance' of him. Right from the start, the church was a sacramental fellowship. Word ('to hear the apostles teach') and sacrament ('to break bread') were held together in a strong combination, the foundation of a church with a vigorous life.

——— *Prayer* ———

'And to pray' is a free translation. The original says that the early Christians continued constantly 'in the prayers'. This, in conjunction with **Acts 2.46**—'They kept up their daily attendance at the temple'—hints broadly at the regular round of corporate temple worship from which they did not divorce themselves but, rather, in which they gladly continued to join. No doubt, over meals at home and under a variety of local needs, the Christians joined also in informal prayer, in twos and threes and in larger groups. It was their 'vital breath'. 'They met constantly to hear . . . to share . . . to break bread . . . to pray.' They needed *God*, and they found him in this fourfold activity. But they also needed *one another*. They needed to meet and to do so constantly, consistently. They knew that a solitary Christian was a contradiction in terms. They were members of a body, the body of Christ. They dared not engage in any form of Christianity which manifested itself in an individualism run riot. They were made for one another, for mutual enrichment, for corporate nourishment. Only so could they *serve*. Only so could they enter into their inheritance as *sons and daughters of God*.

—— ACTS OF THE SPIRIT ——

From its inception, the Christian church was a charismatic body (**1 Corinthians 12.4ff.**). That is to say, it realized that it had been given, in rich variety, gifts (*charismata*) which its members were not to bury in the ground but were to trade with (**Matthew 25.14ff.**) and to use in the *service* of God, of his needy people, of his church. Pentecost, when the Spirit came in power on the disciples gathered in the upper room, was not simply an historic event to which they looked back nostalgically. The Spirit of Pentecost was for every newborn member of the body of Christ, to enable him or her to fulfil the purpose that God had in giving that particular gift to that particular person. Just as 'the Son of Man did not come to be served, but to serve' (**Mark 10.45**) so his followers were committed to a life of service. Just as he by his teaching ministry pushed back the tide of ignorance, and by his preaching ministry pushed back the tide of sin, and by his healing ministry pushed back the tide of sickness and disease (see above, Chapter 6), so were they to engage in a ministry of teaching, preaching, and healing, aiming for the broken to make them whole and the sinful to make them holy.

Paul put it clearly. He was obviously a dynamic and forceful person, and was probably aware of the danger inherent in having such a character. It would have been easy for him to be self-centred in his preaching ministry. So he wrote: 'It is not ourselves that we proclaim; we proclaim Christ Jesus as Lord.' But he knew that in any preaching the human element does come in—and rightly so. What sort of proclamation should *that* be? He is quite clear: we proclaim 'ourselves as your servants for Jesus' sake.' (**2 Corinthians 4.5**) That answer was spot on. The Servant-Son had found in Paul a man who knew that God's purpose for his world and for his church would only be fulfilled through human beings who incarnated the spirit of servanthood which had been the supreme mark of the life and teaching of the master. So Paul delighted to speak of himself as a '*minister of the gospel*' (**Ephesians 3.7; Colossians 1.23**), a 'servant of the church' (**Colossians 1.25**); his whole person and work unreservedly put to the service of Jesus' cause.

——— TASK OF THE CHURCH ———

It would be an interesting exercise to work through the Acts of the Apostles and to see how, in fact, this carrying forward of Christ's servant ministry worked out in the lives and conduct of the members of the early church. Clearly, *teaching* and *preaching* took an important place. We see Peter, who only a short while previously had, at the sneer of a servant-girl, denied his Lord, now preaching fearlessly to the crowds (**Acts 2.14ff.; 3.11ff.**). He, and John too, were 'uneducated laymen' (**Acts 4.13**), but companionship with Jesus and the wind and fire of Pentecost gave their rough words great power. So it was with Stephen, the first martyr, the man with a face like that of an angel and no doubt with a tongue to match (**Acts 6.8–7.60**). And when Saul of Tarsus, persecutor turned apostle, brought his gifts of mind and heart to the service of the word, the church was built up. No doubt many who might not have been touched by the approach of a Galilean tradesman were captivated by the more intellectual approach of this cultured man who was able to understand their outlook. Scholarship warmed with the flame of Pentecost was a powerful weapon.

Jesus, as we have seen, preached and taught. But he also healed. His early followers knew that he had called them to a healing ministry, and they were not forgetful of the fact that service includes the physical and the mental as well as the spiritual. The gospel is addressed to the health of the *whole* person. We do not have to go far into the book of Acts before we find Peter and John confronted by a cripple begging by the temple gate. Peter has no financial resources with which to help him, but 'what I have I give you: in the name of Jesus Christ of Nazareth, get up and walk.' (**Acts 3.1–10**)

'Gifts of healing' occupy an honoured place in Paul's list of gifts of the Spirit given in **1 Corinthians 12.4ff.** When the church has been at its best, it has gone to the world as a healing body, conscious of the fact that human beings are a unity of body, mind, and spirit, and that God's purpose for each individual is that he or she should be a *whole* person. The gift of healing which God has given to his church has often been abused (have we not all seen, at least on our television screens, the rantings of so-called healers, in the setting of noisy campaigns?) But the abuse of a lovely thing does not mean that we take no part in the thing itself. We are committed to a healing ministry. Teaching, preaching, and healing go together; what God has joined together let no one put asunder!

The early church was a down-to-earth church. Its members were followers of one who had come down to earth. The incarnation was no airy-fairy affair; it had to do with flesh and blood; with sickness and health; with family relationships; with finance (see, for example, how much care Paul gave to a financial appeal for people who had run into difficulties in Jerusalem: **2 Corinthians 8–9**). 'Ourselves your servants for Jesus' sake'—servants of the Servant-Son—it was a splendid stance to take.

——— GOD'S SONS AND DAUGHTERS ———

So far, so good—very good! However, we have said much about servanthood and little about sonship. Left by itself, the idea of servanthood *might* suggest servility, though that is by no means inherent in the biblical use of the idea. We must balance it with the concept of sonship. That is why the title of this book has a hyphen in it—the Servant-Son.

Let us sketch an imaginary scene. You are in Galilee, and you have been among the crowd to whom Jesus has been ministering. He has been acting as servant through preaching to them, teaching them, healing them. It has been strenuous though delightful work. Now evening has come and the crowds at last have dispersed. Jesus, weary but deeply satisfied, is going off into the hills, for sleep and renewal of body, mind, and spirit. He is alone—and so are you. Dare you have a brief word with him? You decide to take the risk, for you have something you long to ask him. I imagine something like this taking place:

You: Teacher, you're tired. But may I hold you up just for a few minutes?

Jesus: Yes, of course.

You: I have been watching you at work all day long. I have been in the crowd listening to you, and I have seen how everyone has been hanging on your words. There is no doubt you have been serving them wonderfully. What is your secret? How do you do it? How do you keep serene when the crowds press in on you? How do you—well, I hardly know how to put it—make broken people whole?

Jesus: I have a wonderful father. It is *his* work that I do. We work together. We are in closest touch with each other. I am his *son*. When I pray, I use the most intimate word to address him—'Abba, father'. My father knows my needs. This being so, the stress goes; the power flows. It is good to be a servant. It is wonderful to be a son.

In this imaginary scene, I do not think we have strayed far from the picture given us in Scripture: the picture of the adolescent boy in the temple—'In my father's house', about my father's business, among my father's people (**Luke 2.49**); the picture of Jesus teaching his disciples how to pray—'This is how you should pray: Our Father in heaven . . .' (**Matthew 6.9ff.**); the picture of Jesus telling people how they should live, carefree—'Your heavenly Father knows . . .' (**Matthew 6.32**); the picture of Jesus sharing in the work on which his father is engaged—'My Father continues to work, and I must work too.' (**John 5.17**) There is something royal about such a father-son relationship.

It is precisely this relationship which the son invites us to share with him. We are adopted into the family of God, and the Spirit there given us is not one of slavery but, on the contrary, one that enables us to cry out joyfully, just as Jesus did, 'Abba, father!' It is almost too good to be true, but 'the Spirit of God affirms to our spirit that we *are* God's children; and if children, then heirs, heirs of God and fellow-heirs with Christ.' (**Romans 8.16–17**, author's italics) 'It is through faith that you are all sons of God in union with Christ Jesus.' (**Galatians 3.26**)

This intimacy of relationship between a rich father and his children is so astonishing that John can scarcely believe it. He has to repeat it, to let it sink in—'Consider how great is the love which the Father has bestowed on us in calling us his children! For that is what we are . . . Dear friends, we are now God's children . . .' (**1 John 3.1,2**)

The unknown writer of the Epistle to the Hebrews approaches this family relationship from another angle, and again we can detect amazement that this is so. In chapter 2, Jesus is described as the 'pioneer' of our salvation and as our *brother*! 'He does not shrink'— he might well have done so—'he does not shrink from calling men his brothers.' (**Hebrews 2.11**) Jesus shared in our flesh and blood, he broke the power of death and liberated us from servitude—he was 'made like his brothers in every way.' (**Hebrews 2.14–17**)

Brothers and sisters of Christ! We should hesitate to accept such a concept, perhaps, had it not been hinted at clearly in a saying of Jesus himself. Mark depicts Jesus as 'looking round at those who were sitting in the circle about him', that is to say, at those eager to hear and attend to his word, and saying 'Here are my mother and my brothers. Whoever does the will of God is my brother and sister and mother.' (**Mark 3.34–35**)

Servant-sons—we note that hyphen; we mark that balance. *Servants—so our heads are kept down*, our shoulders bent to the task of sharing, as Jesus did, the load of human sin and suffering, ignorance, and disease, and all the ills that flesh is heir to. We cannot preach the gospel and leave social service to others; social service is part of the gospel. Ordination and foot-washing go together. Keen minds which know no evading of difficult issues and dirty hands which carry others' loads are joined in a holy alliance. Servants of God and your servants for Jesus' sake. *Sons—so our heads are held high.* Sons and daughters of the Most High! Brothers and sisters of Christ! Members of the Body of Christ! 'A royal house of priests for our God', reigning on earth (**Revelation 5.10**).

—— *QUESTIONS* ——

1 The four points of **Acts 2.42** provide a good pattern for the life of a church. At which of these points is your church strong/weak?

2 Healing was an integral part of our Lord's commission to his church (**Luke 9.2** and elsewhere). Can you give up-to-date instances of the church's obedience to the commission? Are there some in your vicinity?

3 We often think of Jesus as Lord and Saviour. What difference would it make if we frequently thought of him, and prayed to him, as our brother?

4 'I admire Jesus. I won't touch the church.' How would you help someone who said that to you?

—— PRAYERS ——

Give us grace, O Lord, to live each day
   as if it were the day of your coming.
May we be urgent to prepare your way
   by fighting all evil,
   by preaching the gospel,
   by feeding the hungry,
   by releasing the oppressed,
   and by healing the sick.
So may we hasten the triumph of your Kingdom,
   and bring glory to your name.[1]

Most gracious Father, we most humbly beseech thee for thy holy catholic Church. Fill it with all truth; in all truth with all peace. Where it is corrupt, purge it; where it is in error, direct it; where anything is amiss, reform it; where it is right, strengthen and confirm it; where it is in want, furnish it; where it is divided, heal it, and unite it in thy love; through Jesus Christ our Lord.[2]

Eternal God,
   let this mind be in us which was also in Christ Jesus,
   that, as he from his loftiness stooped to the death of the cross,
   so we in our lowliness may humble ourselves,
      believing,
      obeying,
      living and dying,
for his name's sake.[3]

It is the purpose of God that we should 'share the likeness of his Son'—here and now.
Glory to the Father for such a plan.
Glory to the Son for such a pattern.

THE SERVANT-SON

Glory to the Spirit for such an empowering.
Glory be to God on high
  and on earth peace, peace and blessing without end.

        This day, dear Lord, and every day,
          make me faithful as your servant
          and joyful as your son (daughter).

Jesus—Then and Now

In the previous chapters, we have been thinking of the Servant-Son as he was *then*, in the years of his youth and ministry.

In this chapter, we ask whether we may speak of him in the present tense—as he is *now*. Is he just a memory? Or is he more than that? If so, of what does that 'more' consist?

Is a meeting with him possible? Is it possible even to live life in his presence? Does he still come to us, address us, confront us? If so, how does that encounter take place?

Two stories of Jesus' appearance after his resurrection will help us in our quest:

> **Luke 24.13–53**
> **John 20.19–29**

In this book so far, we have been concerned primarily with Jesus as he was when he walked the highways and byways of Palestine in the opening decades of the first century.

We have watched him against the background of the Jewish people in thrall to the Roman conqueror, developing as a young man at home, at his trade, obedient to the constraints to which all of his people were subject (Chapter 1). We have watched him at his baptism in the Jordan (Chapter 2) and at his temptation in the wilderness (Chapter 3). We have glanced at the four servant songs of Isaiah which we believe were formative in his concept of himself as the servant of the Lord (Chapter 4). We have lingered with him at the synagogue when he preached his first sermon and, in doing so, defined his mission, hoisted his flag (Chapter 5). We have spent a considerable time imagining him entering into a developing relationship with God, as at once his father and his king. That relationship was the key to his emphasis on the reign (kingdom) of God. We noted that his work had a *negative* aspect to it—the battle against ignorance, sin, and disease—and a *positive* aspect—the achievement of 'peace', integration of personality, wholeness, holiness, the welfare of society; to this end he taught, and preached, and healed (Chapter 6). Nor did he confine himself to words alone—he delighted in dramatizing his message (Chapter 7).

A figure has emerged from our study, the figure of a young man—he died when he was about thirty-three—who came to see himself both as a servant of the Lord and as son of the Most High. *That* duality—note the hyphen in Servant-Son—was the essence of his being and of his mission. That was to be the essential mission of his followers. For throughout his ministry he had been engaged in training a body of people who would pursue his work when his physical presence with them had ceased to be—his body, there to pray and preach and heal and witness, there to leaven society; it was a sinning body, but endowed with the Spirit (Chapter 8).

—— JESUS THEN ——

As we have worked together, we have been engaged on a fascinating task. To look back on Jesus' story, as it has emerged chapter by chapter, is to be inspired. After all, life is like that: we gain our ideals from the stories of giants whom we have had as our heroes—they have inspired us. Hence the immense power of biography. The men and women who form the subjects of such books, being dead, yet speak. 'If only I could be like him—make music as she did—lead as Churchill did—heal as Florence Nightingale did . . .' 'If only'—the story or the memory of a life can be an inspiration. On the other hand, the reading of a biography can lead to a barren nostalgia, even to regret, at worst to remorse—'but I am *not* like that, nor ever shall be.'

We look back with an immense thankfulness to the figure we have tried to sketch in these chapters. The record of that life is, surely, unique. Jesus stands alone, with a majesty all his own. 'Thanks for the memory . . .' But can we leave it at that? Never! Even as I write, I have slipped from the past tense into the present: 'He *stands* alone . . .' There must be another chapter to this book. We have been engaged with Jesus *then*. Dare we, should we speak of Jesus *now*? The sub-title 'Jesus Then and Now' suggests that we may.

If we begin with the New Testament—and we can hardly begin elsewhere—we find that there is no note of nostalgia in its pages. Some of us were brought up on a hymn whose opening verse ran:

> I think when I read that sweet story of old,
>> When Jesus was here among men,
> How he bade little children to come to his side,
>> I should like to *have been with him then*.

That is an understandable sentiment, but it does not spring from the early records.

The stories which the evangelists tell of the appearances of Jesus to his friends after his resurrection have an air of mystery about them which we cannot fully understand. What was the nature of his risen body? How did he appear?—and disappear? We must be content to leave some questions open and unanswered. But one thing stands out clearly: those disciples did not live on a memory. They were confronted with a presence. This was the authentic Jesus whom they had known and worked with. This was the crucified Jesus with the marks of suffering in his hands and side. This was the Jesus who could be recognized by the particular way in which he broke the bread at a supper party (Luke 24.35). They could not mistake the voice that said: 'Peace be with you' (John 20.19, 21). But now there was a vibrancy about him which seemed to be independent of the erstwhile restraints of time and space. And when the forty days of post-resurrection appearances were behind them and his physical presence was withdrawn, 'I will be with you always, to the end of time' seemed the statement of a living reality rather than the expression of a vague hope.

When we pass from the gospels to the stories of the early church recorded in the Acts of the Apostles, there is no nostalgia here. Rather, there is the experience of a very powerful, though unseen, presence among the disciples of Jesus. It is to Jesus that Stephen, the dying martyr, commends his spirit. To Jesus Stephen appeals not to hold their sin against those who were killing him (Acts 7.59–60). So real was the presence of the risen Lord that the early disciples, staunch monotheists that they were, when they prayed, prayed naturally to *him*. He was not dead. He was not a mere memory. He was alive.

So it was that, when they continued his healing work, it was in his 'name', in the power of his presence, that they healed. They had to insist that it was no power or godliness of their own that brought about health (Acts 3.1–16; we note the repetition of 'the name of Jesus' in Acts 3.6, 16). And when at last Saul of Tarsus came to lay down the arms of his rebellion, he found himself in a one-to-one encounter. 'Tell me, Lord, who you are . . .' 'I am Jesus, whom you are persecuting' (Acts 9.3–5) Then, when he went on his missionary travels, he went 'commissioned . . . by Jesus Christ and God the Father who raised him from the dead' (Galatians 1.1) and he greeted the readers of his letter to the Galatians with the words: 'Grace to you and peace from God the Father and our Lord Jesus Christ.' (Galatians 1.3) It was an extraordinary juxtaposition—the father and the Lord Jesus joining in the benediction!

In the same letter to the Galatians, Paul includes a little bit of autobiography which brilliantly illustrates the point we are seeking to make. He is writing of the life he is now living, the rigorous life of a travelling emissary of Jesus. He calls his master 'the Son of God who loved me and gave himself up for me'. In that phrase he looked back to that point in history, very recent history, when a man hung on a gibbet outside Jerusalem's wall. It was the great dividing point of history. But to Paul it was more than that. He could only express its meaning in personal terms—the son of God and me: 'he loved *me* and gave himself up for *me*.' What did it mean to him? What was it—a memory? Yes, of course. But *so much more*. His verbs slip into the *present* tense: 'The life I now live is not my life, but the *life which Christ lives in me*, and my present mortal life is lived by faith in the Son of God . . .' (**Galatians 2.20**, author's italics) No dead Christ here! No nostalgia here! On the contrary, a present lively reality which is life-enhancing and life-transforming.

As we read in the New Testament, in practically all of its strata, we find ourselves not in the presence of a memory but of a person who commissions, heals, empowers; a person who can be known and prayed to and, above all, a person who loves and can be loved. We must use *both* tenses—Jesus *was*, in the reality of the person who formed the basis of our studies in Chapters 1–7. He *is*—in the power of his risen life. Yes: and he *will be* to the end of time, and beyond. This is the Servant-Son, risen, ascended, glorified.

—— *JESUS NOW* ——

The experience of the church over nearly two millennia adds its 'Amen' to what we have said. At its best, the church has kept Jesus the Servant-Son at the centre of its worship and of its proclamation. It had to delay for a while before it could spell out its belief in the form of creeds, of the threefold being of God as Father, Son, and Spirit. Indeed each new generation must address itself to this task afresh, for we shall always be finding new depths in these eternal truths. But at the heart of our belief stands the figure of the Servant-Son, offering his grace, 'the grace of our Lord Jesus Christ', making his demands, summoning, sending, accompanying. His 'other self', the Holy Spirit of Jesus, is always at the ready to succour and sustain.

Albert Schweitzer (1875–1965) is famous for many things—he was musician, missionary doctor at Lambarene, theologian, and

Nobel prizewinner. Of his writings, perhaps the best known is a book written when he was thirty—*The Quest of the Historical Jesus.*[1] His closing sentences have been quoted over and over again. He is writing of Jesus:

> He comes to us as one unknown, without a name, as of old, by the lakeside, he said to those men who knew him not. He speaks to us the same word: 'Follow thou me!' and sets us to the tasks which he has to fulfil for our time. He commands. And to those who obey him, whether they be wise or simple, he will reveal himself in the toils, the conflicts, the sufferings which they shall pass through in his fellowship, and, as an ineffable mystery, they shall learn in their own experience, who he is.

Those are noble words. They have about them the ring of truth. We note those present tenses: 'He comes . . . he speaks . . . he sets us to do tasks . . . he commands.' Yes: and there is a future tense as well: 'He will reveal himself.' For this is no merely historic figure, no static Christ. He has a way of striding on ahead and we must run if we are to keep up with him. This is the dynamic Christ.

'He comes to us'—comes as love, and with the patient insistence which is the mark of love. Such love never despairs of us, but goes on seeking till it finds its loved one.

He comes to us—in the intimacy of personal encounter, loving us as if there were only one of us to love. The ninety-and-nine must wait; I alone matter. His message comes not in the form of a circular letter or an encyclical. It is personally addressed to me and, miracle of miracles, it is signed 'Yours ever'. Love seeks a response—always.

> O Love that wilt not let me go,
> I rest my weary soul on thee:
> I give thee back the life I owe,
> That in thine ocean depths its flow
>   May richer, fuller, be.[2]

It is understandable that at times we should long for some physical manifestation of his presence, rather as Mary Magdalene wanted to hold on to Jesus in her encounter with him after his resurrection (**John 20.11–18**). The hymn writer was conscious of that desire but not daunted by it:

> Jesus, these eyes have never seen
> That radiant form of thine;
> The veil of sense hangs dark between
> Thy blessed face and mine.
>
> I see thee not, I hear thee not,
> Yet art thou oft with me;
> And earth hath ne'er so dear a spot
> As when I meet with thee.
>
> Yet, though I have not seen, and still
> Must rest in faith alone,
> I love thee, dearest Lord, and will
> Unseen, but not unknown.[3]

That gets pretty close to the truth.

It was this intimacy of personal encounter that meant so much to the Servant-Son himself. He made a point of withdrawing from the busyness of daily life into the silence of the hills, there to meet with his father (see, for example, **Mark 1.35; 2.13; 3.7**). His use of the word *Abba* points to a close relationship between father and Servant-Son. Love calls for nurturing—even a marriage-relationship can grow arid, or even break, if it is not nourished and cared for. Jesus knew that. The Servant-Son was able to commit himself into the hands of his father-God at the end of his life because all through that life he had cultivated that relationship. Then, at the end, death could not break it.

The Servant-Son bids us share that special *Abba* relationship with him, not at some distant time when this life is over, but in the humdrum and demanding experiences of everyday life.

He comes to us—in the community of his people. The Servant-Son grew and developed not in isolation, but among a worshipping community. He may sometimes have found the weekly worship of the synagogue dry and uninspiring. He probably did. No doubt at other times he found it stimulating. But, good or bad as his experience of synagogue worship might be, he found himself exposed there to the influence of the Scriptures, to the help of common prayer, to the warmth of the fellowship of his Jewish relatives and friends. When, more rarely, he went up to Jerusalem, he found the worship of the great temple raising in his mind many questions, even doubts (see Chapter 1). But there again, he could learn from his seniors. There again he could glimpse something of the majesty of God. There again he could mix, to his great profit, with God's people. God came to him in the worship of the synagogue and temple, and the Servant-Son grew as a member of a believing community.

When it came to planning for the future of his work, Jesus knew that he could not do it alone. So 'he appointed twelve *to be his companions* . . .' (**Mark 3.14**, author's italics). They needed his companionship if they were to learn to grow. But he needed *their* companionship. He did not want to face his task in solitude—that would be more lonely than he could bear. And he found that his *Abba*-God revealed himself often in the fellowship of a *community* as he could not fully do in solitary meeting. In the Servant-Son's encounter with his twelve, wayward as they often were, God came to him.

The promise holds true: 'Where two or three meet together in my name, I am there among them.' (**Matthew 18.20**)

He comes to us—in the sacraments of his love. We have seen something of what his baptism meant to the Servant-Son (Chapter 2). The opening of the heavens and the descent of the Spirit like a dove (**Matthew 3.16**) were a dramatizing of that divine love which takes the initiative in God's coming to his people. And it is surely of the deepest significance that when Jesus wanted to assure his fear-full disciples of his never-failing presence, he did it by bidding them to a meal, and pouring out the wine and breaking the bread in their presence. 'Do this as a memorial of me' (**Luke 22.19**)—the Eucharist has been, and is, to the faithful supremely the meeting-place where God provides food for his people and they respond in thanksgiving and faith. The Christ of the Last Supper comes to us, meets us, nourishes us, equips us for the battle.

He comes to us—in the fires of temptation. When we were considering the temptation of Jesus in the wilderness (Chapter 3) we noticed Luke's strange phrase 'led by the Spirit and tempted by the devil' (**Luke 4.2**). It was a Servant-Son 'full of the Holy Spirit' who returned from the baptism and ventured out into the wilderness. But who is to deny that it was a *stronger* Servant-Son who emerged from the wilderness after those fearful forty days? Temptation is never to be sought, for we are weak and fallible creatures. But when it comes, as come it does to all God's people, God can take it and, in giving us victory over it, can make us the stronger, the more understanding, for its experience. We cannot doubt that in Jesus' encounter with the devil, there was also an encounter with God. Jesus' *Abba*-God came to him in the wilderness. The Servant-Son comes to us in the fires of temptation. You remember that old tyrant Nebuchadnezzar, who dispatched three men of God to the fiery furnace. On looking into the blaze, he said: 'Was it not three men whom we threw bound into the fire? . . . Yet . . . I can see four men walking about in the fire, free and unharmed; and the fourth *looks like a god*.' (**Daniel 3.24–25**, author's italics)

He comes to us—in the Scriptures. Again and again the Servant-Son found that the Scriptures (what Christians call the Old Testament) were a meeting-place where he could encounter God. With words from those Scriptures he rebutted attacks of the tempter (Chapter 3). On a passage from **Isaiah 61** he based his first sermon at Nazareth (Chapter 5). The servant songs of Isaiah were formative in giving shape to his ministry leading up to the cross (Chapter 4). Quotations from the Psalms were on his lips as he died. We need not elaborate this theme.

As we approach the Bible, we should do so with our critical faculties fully alert. We should use to the limit all the aids which the biblical scholars can provide. But all this will be of little avail unless we submit ourselves to the judgement of Scripture; allow ourselves to be criticized by Scripture; reach the point where, in the mercy of God, we find ourselves *addressed by him* as we 'read, mark, learn, and inwardly digest' the Scriptures.[4]

On the road to Emmaus, the risen Servant-Son 'explained' to the couple who walked with him 'in the whole of Scripture the things that referred to himself' (**Luke 24.27**). As they looked back on that never-to-be-forgotten journey, they said to one another: 'Were not our hearts on fire as he talked with us on the road and explained the

Scriptures to us?' **(Luke 24.32)** That is authentic Bible study. It leads to mental illumination. It warms the heart. It issues in action—'Without a moment's delay they set out and returned to Jerusalem', found the disciples and said, 'It is true: the Lord has risen . . .' **(Luke 24.32–34)**

He comes to us—in the service of human need. One great principle seems to have motivated the Servant-Son in his ministry. It was the doing of his father's will in the service of his father's children. 'Your kingdom come, your will be done'—this to him was basic. So he prayed **(Matthew 6.10)**. So he lived: 'The Son of Man did not come to be served but to serve, and to give his life a ransom for many.' **(Mark 10.45)** In this he found his deepest satisfaction: 'For me it is meat and drink to do the will of him who sent me until I have finished his work.' **(John 4.34)** Such ministry was life-enhancing to him, as it was life-giving to others. It was the service of love: 'He had always loved his own who were in the world, and he loved them to the end.' **(John 13.1)**

Jesus comes to his church and bids us join him in the ministry of health, in the service of love. He was sent, so he told his people in the Nazareth synagogue, to 'the poor . . . the prisoners . . . the blind . . . the broken victims . . .' **(Luke 4.18)** 'As the Father sent me, *so* I send you.' **(John 20.21,** author's italics) It is in the heart of this ministry to human need that we find Jesus—he comes to us *there*. It is a grubby meeting-place, sometimes a bloody one. But we meet him *there*. 'Anything you did for one of my brothers here, however insignificant, you did for me.' **(Matthew 25.40)**

He comes to us—Schweitzer was right. A relationship is established between the Servant-Son and his servant-sons and servant-daughters which deepens and matures as life goes on. Jesus comes to us invitingly—'Let us enter into a relationship together.' That is the essence of the Christian religion—the word 'religion' most probably arises from a Latin word meaning to bind together. 'Let us be bound together in an indissoluble relationship', he would say, 'A relationship not of a cosy or selfish religiosity, but one which binds us into the fellowship of the body of Christ, committed as it is to its saving mission to the world.' It is an invitation to be received with open hands and thankful hearts.

There was nothing airy-fairy about the relationship between the

Servant-Son and his father. It was very down-to-earth. The maturing of it had to be worked for—I had almost written 'practised'—if it was to deepen and mature, as indeed it did. It was developed in a life of rough-and-tumble experiences—among the tensions of a big family, in the stresses of trade and commerce, among the pressures and smells of sweating crowds, in the terrors of a public trial, and in the horrors of a rugged cross.

For most of us our discipleship will mature not in the seclusion of a Trappist monastery (though those who adopt the monastic life assure us that it has tensions and trials of its own), but in the circumstances of ordinary living. Are there any pointers to set us on the way? I would mention three, with no apology for their 'elementariness', for we are all beginners in that relationship which potentially begins at our baptism and eventually transcends the barriers of death:

—— Focusing on Jesus ——

I take it for granted that servant-sons and servant-daughters recognize that some moments must be carved out of every day when they can be alone with God. But who are we to approach 'the blessed and only Sovereign, King of kings and Lord of lords', who 'alone possesses immortality, dwelling in unapproachable light' (1 Timothy 6.15–16)? We might well hesitate. But God has been focused for us in Jesus, the Servant-Son, and we may focus on *him*. In him, the image of God is clear and we can look to him and at him again and again. 'In him God in all his fullness chose to dwell.' (Colossians 1.19) 'Anyone who has seen me has seen the Father.' (John 14.9)

—— Referral to Jesus ——

By this I mean seeking the mind of Jesus on the *major* choices and decisions of our lives; seeking his will rather than our own on the choice of life-partner, work, leisure, on the control of ambitions, hopes, fears, worries.

I mean the referral to Jesus of the *minor* affairs of everyday living—relationships with our family, with friends, the writing of letters, the conduct of conversations. Cultivating the habit of arrow-prayers will ensure the growth of referral to Jesus of things great and small.

———— *Silence with Jesus* ————

The most important part of prayer is not the broadcasting of our needs to him. It may well be simply keeping quiet in his presence. Consciously holding oneself there can be revolutionary, character-forming. It can lead to a sharing in the likeness of Jesus—which is God's purpose for his children (**Romans 8. 29**)

When a husband and wife have lived together for many years, they do not need to fill every space in their lives with a barrage of conversation. Simply to *be together* in silence is enough. The meaning of that little parable does not need to be pressed. But it is one of the ways in which servant-sons and servant-daughters are made.

———— *JESUS—THEN AND NOW* ————

In the early part of 1994 there was held a series of six lunch-hour meetings in the city of Winchester. Each lasted half an hour. The meetings were ecumenical. The title of the addresses was *Jesus—then and now*. We sought to look at the person of the young man from Nazareth whose coming was to be of untold blessing to his own generation and to succeeding ones worldwide.

It would, I think, be true to say that as we looked at him, he returned our gaze. Our eyes met, as it were. He presented himself to us—inviting us to let him take us on, to refashion us, to make us whole (holy). He looked for our response.

But how was that response to be made? The speaker did an unusual thing. He suggested that those who wished might return the look of Jesus in gratitude, uttering two words only: 'Yours—*truly*' (to be, to worship, to give, to work, to suffer, to enjoy, to rejoice). 'Truly' was the operative word.

The speaker dared to assert that Jesus would answer those words with two of his own: 'Yours—*ever*'. The vow 'Yours—truly' was accepted. The promise was given: 'Yours—*ever*'. It has never yet been broken. 'I will be with you always, to the end of time'.

—— *QUESTIONS* ——

1 Imagine that you were one of the two people who walked with Jesus to Emmaus (**Luke 24.13**). You shared a Bible study with him (**Luke 24.13–27**); you shared a meal with him (**Luke 24.28–32**). What does the story suggest for:

> your own devotional life?
> the public worship of the Church?

2 In John's story of Jesus' appearance after his resurrection, he mentions Jesus' dramatic action in breathing on the disciples (**John 20.22**). This reminds us of **Genesis 2.7** and of **2 Corinthians 5.17**. Do you see the connection? How does it impinge on you as a servant-son/daughter of God?

3 When the early Christians looked to God in prayer, it seemed to them that they saw the face of Jesus. Indeed, they often addressed their prayers to him. What does this suggest to you? Would it help to think of Jesus as the point where God was *focused* for them? Discuss this.

4 'He comes to us.' We have outlined six ways in which the Servant-Son comes to us (pp. 112–17). Would you like to add further ways to the list? Which makes the strongest appeal to *you*?

—— PRAYERS ——

Speak to Him thou for He hears, and Spirit with Spirit can meet—
Closer is He than breathing, and nearer than hands and feet.[5]

Thanks be to God!

Whenever we come to the Lord in prayer, we do so in the assurance
that he is present with us. We do not have to seek his presence. We
are daily living in his presence. So in our moments of prayer we may
know that we are speaking to one who is near and not far off, whose
love is all around us and who understands our every need.[6]

Thanks be to God—again!

Breathe on me, Breath of God,
Fill me with life anew,
That I may love what thou dost love,
And do what thou wouldst do.[7]

O Lord Jesus Christ, thou Word and Revelation of the Eternal
Father, come, we pray thee, take possession of our hearts and reign
where thou hast right to reign. So fill our minds with the thought and
our imaginations with the picture of thy love, that there may be in us
no room for any desire that is discordant with thy holy will. Cleanse
us, we pray thee, from all that may make us deaf to thy call or slow
to obey it, who, with the Father and the Holy Spirit art one God,
blessed for ever.[8]

O Jesus, Master Carpenter of Nazareth, who on the cross through
wood and nails hast wrought man's full salvation: wield well thy
tools in this thy workshop, that we who come to thee rough-hewn

may be fashioned to a truer beauty by thy hand, who with the Father and the Holy Spirit livest one God world without end.

Day by day, dear Lord, three things of thee we pray:
 to see thee more clearly,
 follow thee more nearly,
 love thee more dearly

day by day.

NOTES

All biblical quotations are from the *Revised English Bible*, Oxford University Press and Cambridge University Press, 1989, unless otherwise indicated.

Chapter 1

1. Edmund Digby Buxton, *Prayer Plus*, Churchman Publishing, 1993, p. 27.
2. *The Alternative Service Book 1980* (by permission of the Central Board of Finance of the Church of England), p. 300.

Chapter 2

1. A prayer of discharged prisoners—Acts 4.29–30.
2. Collect of The Birth of John the Baptist, ASB, p. 777.
3. ASB, p. 258.
4. Patrick Appleford, *100 Hymns for Today*, no. 58.
5. Collect of Epiphany 1, ASB, p. 463.

Chapter 3

1. Frank Colquhoun (ed.), *New Parish Prayers*, (by permission of Hodder & Stoughton, 1982), p. 50.
2. Collect of Lent 1, ASB, p. 504.
3. Based on Paul's prayer in Philippians 1.9–10.
4. Ted Loder, *Guerillas of Grace, Prayers for the Battle*, (Lura Media, San Diego, California, 1984), p. 54.
5. Loder, *Guerillas of Grace*, p. 132.

Chapter 4

1. Collect of Pentecost 10, ASB, p. 683.
2. Collect of Advent 2, ASB, p. 426.
3. Colquhoun, *New Parish Prayers*, p. 136.
4. Colquhoun, *New Parish Prayers*, p. 138.
5. Source unknown.

NOTES

Chapter 5

1. Adapted from Bishop George Ridding's *A Litany of Remembrance*, (George Allen & Unwin Ltd., [1905], 1942).

Chapter 6

1. 1 Thessalonians 5.23–24.

Chapter 7

1. Frank Colquhoun (ed.), *Parish Prayers*, (by permission of Hodder & Stoughton, 1967), p. 267.
2. Colquhoun, *New Parish Prayers*, p. 108.
3. Loder, *Guerillas of Grace*, pp. 104–105.

Chapter 8

1. M. M. Maddocks, *A Healing House of Prayer*, (by permission of Hodder & Stoughton, 1987), p. 234.
2. Colquhoun, *Parish Prayers*, p. 314.
3. Frank Colquhoun, *My God and King: Prayers of Christian Devotion*, SPCK, 1993, p. 67.

Chapter 9

1. Albert Schweitzer. The Quest of the Historical Jesus, out of print.
2. G. Matheson, *Hymns Ancient and Modern Revised 1950*, (William Clowes & Sons Ltd), no. 359.
3. R. Palmer, *Hymns Ancient and Modern Revised 1950*, no. 347.
4. Collect of Advent 2, ASB pp. 426–7.
5. Alfred, Lord Tennyson, 'The Higher Pantheism' (1847).
6. Colquhoun, *My God and King*, p. 105.
7. *Hymns Ancient and Modern Revised* (William Clowes & Sons, Ltd., 1950), no. 236.
8. William Temple, *Readings in St. John's Gospel*, (MacMillan, 1940), p. 412.

INDEX OF SCRIPTURE REFERENCES